CASE STUDIES: APPLYING EDUCATIONAL PSYCHOLOGY

Dinah L. Jackson
Queens College
Charlotte, North Carolina

Jeanne Ellis Ormrod
University of Northern Colorado

Merrill,
an imprint of Prentice Hall
Upper Saddle River, New Jersey   *Columbus, Ohio*

Library of Congress Cataloging-in-Publication Data

Jackson, Dinah L.
    Case studies: applying educational psychology / Dinah L. Jackson,
Jeanne E. Ormrod.
        p.   cm.
    ISBN 0-13-569120-6
        1. School psychology--United States--Case studies. 2. Educational
    psychology---Case studies. I. Ormrod, Jeanne Ellis. II. Title.
    LB1027.55.J33   1998
    370.15--dc21   97-21726
                                                                            CIP

Cover photo: ©Arthur Tilley/FPG, International
Editor: Kevin M. Davis
Production Editor: Julie Peters
Text Designer: Brenda Dobson
Cover Designer and Coordinator: Karrie M. Converse
Production Manager: Deidra M. Schwartz
Director of Marketing: Kevin Flanagan
Marketing Manager: Suzanne Stanton
Advertising/Marketing Coordinator: Julie Shough

This book was set in Times Roman and was printed and bound by R. R. Donnelley & Sons
Company. The cover was printed by Phoenix Color Corp.

© 1998 by Prentice-Hall, Inc.
Simon & Schuster/A Viacom Company
Upper Saddle River, New Jersey 07458

Printed in the United States of America

10 9 8 7 6 5 4 3 2

ISBN 0-13-569120-6

Prentice-Hall International (UK) Limited, *London*
Prentice-Hall of Australia Pty. Limited, *Sydney*
Prentice-Hall Canada Inc., *Toronto*
Prentice-Hall Hispanoamericana, S.A., *Mexico*
Prentice-Hall of India Private Limited, *New Delhi*
Prentice-Hall of Japan, Inc., *Tokyo*
Simon & Schuster Asia Pte. Ltd., *Singapore*
Editora Prentice-Hall do Brasil, Ltda., *Rio de Janeiro*

PREFACE

We have been teaching undergraduate and graduate courses in educational psychology for a combined total of twenty-five years, and we've been frustrated by the lack of case study books on the market written specifically from the perspective of our own discipline. We've written this book as a way of giving preservice teachers vicarious experiences with real classroom events, and of "situating" the psychological principles and theories that we teach within a variety of classroom contexts.

The book includes cases that illustrate principles related to learning (cognitive psychology, constructivism, social cognitive theory, and behaviorism), motivation (attribution theory, intrinsic motivation), child development (Piaget, Vygotsky, Kohlberg), diversity (cultural and gender differences), and students with special needs (physical disabilities, learning disabilities, mental retardation, emotional disturbance, and traumatic brain injury). It is probably best used as a supplement to a textbook in educational psychology, foundations of education, or learning theories, rather than as a replacement for one.

Collaborating together, we have brought somewhat different strengths to the book. Dinah Jackson has seventeen years' experience in K–12 settings, first as a second-grade teacher, then as a kindergarten teacher, later as a junior high school English teacher, and eventually as a teacher of students with special needs at the elementary, middle, and secondary school levels. Jeanne Ormrod has taught middle school social studies and worked as a school psychologist.

Each of the cases we present here is a true story. Many of the events we describe took place in Dinah's classes, a few took place in Jeanne's classes, and the remainder happened to our colleagues and their students. Naturally, we've changed all of the names to maintain confidentiality, and in some cases we've changed a few details to enhance readability.

Special Features of the Book

Each case study is followed by a series of discussion questions that can help the reader relate classroom events to psychological principles. Accompanying the book is an *Instructor's Manual* that includes a variety of perspectives on how these questions might be answered. The manual also includes a matrix that relates each case study to the psychological theories and principles that it illustrates.

Field Testing of the Cases

We've recently field-tested most of the case studies with students in Dinah's undergraduate educational psychology classes. Students' responses to the cases have been overwhelmingly positive. Here are some examples of the feedback that students have given us:

> "I love the case studies 'cause they are real!"

> "They (the case studies) make me feel like I am in the classroom."

> "It's easy to see how the theories work when I read the case studies. It makes me feel like a real teacher, and this class isn't some hoop that I have to go through to get my degree."

> "The case studies help me focus on the main topics in the textbook. They help make the textbook more real—like what actual teachers would see."

> "The case studies are interesting and help me a lot for real-world situations."

Acknowledgments

Although we are listed as the sole authors of this book, we have hardly written it by ourselves. We would like to express our deepest gratitude to the many students and colleagues who, just by being themselves, have given us so many insights into human cognition and behavior. Our editor, Kevin Davis, has been supportive throughout the development, writing, and production of the book, and his insights on both educational psychology as a discipline and current needs in the market have been invaluable.

D.L.J. and J.E.O.
Greeley, Colorado

TABLE OF CONTENTS

Child and Adolescent Development

(K–2)	Case 1	The Goldfish	1
(K–2)	Case 2	Learning the Ropes	3
(K–2)	Case 3	The Paycheck	7
(3–5)	Case 4	The Art Box	9
(3–5)	Case 5	The Emergency Telephone Call	13
(3–5)	Case 6	Houses and Boats	17
(6–8)	Case 7	Alabama	19
(6–8)	Case 8	Friends	23
(9–12)	Case 9	Pollution	25
(9–12)	Case 10	Studying French	29

Learning and Cognition

(K–2)	Case 11	The Reflection in the Window	33
(K–2)	Case 12	The Marble Jar	35
(K–2)	Case 13	The Morning Routine	37
(3–5)	Case 14	Culture Shock	39
(3–5)	Case 15	A Silent World	43
(3–5)	Case 16	Seven Chips	47
(3–5)	Case 17	The Distracting Influence	51
(3–5)	Case 18	Throwing Tantrums	55
(6–8)	Case 19	Keeping Track of Business	59
(6–8)	Case 20	Summer School	63
(6–8)	Case 21	Topography	67
(6–8)	Case 22	Climate	71
(6–8)	Case 23	Solving Problems	75
(6–8)	Case 24	Consequences	79
(9–12)	Case 25	First Aid	83
(9–12)	Case 26	The Respiratory System	87
(9–12)	Case 27	Coming Back to School	91
(9–12)	Case 28	The Concept Maps	95

Motivation

(K–2)	Case 29	The Star Chart	97
(3–5)	Case 30	The Bulletin Board	99
(3–5)	Case 31	Getting a Drink	101
(6–8)	Case 32	Math Baseball	103
(6–8)	Case 33	The Perfectionist	105
(9–12)	Case 34	Cheerleading Tryouts	107

Classroom Management

(K–2)	Case 35	Letters	111
(3–5)	Case 36	Halloween	115
(6–8)	Case 37	The Stand-up Comic	117
(9–12)	Case 38	Proofreading	121

Instruction and Assessment

(3–5)	Case 39	Horses and Aliens	125
(3–5)	Case 40	Endangered Species	129
(6–8)	Case 41	The Research Paper	133
(9–12)	Case 42	Under the Bleachers	135
(9–12)	Case 43	*The Pearl*	139

Matrix

	K-2	3-5	6-8	9-12	Piaget	Info. Proc. Development	Vygotsky	Social Development	Moral Development	Personal Dev./Erikson	Self-efficacy/Self-esteem	Language Development	Diversity	Special Needs	Class Conditioning	Operant Conditioning	Info. Processing	Knowledge Construction	Complex Cognitive Proc.
The Pearl			✓															✓	
Under the Bleachers			✓																
The Research Paper		✓					✓				✓		✓						
Endangered Species	✓																✓		✓
Horses and Aliens	✓																		
Proofreading		✓									✓			✓					
The Stand-up Comic		✓						✓	✓					✓					
Halloween	✓											✓							
Letters	✓											✓						✓	✓
Cheerleading Tryouts			✓																
The Perfectionist		✓											✓						
Math Baseball		✓							✓										
Getting a Drink	✓							✓		✓									
The Bulletin Board	✓								✓							✓			
The Star Chart	✓								✓										
The Concept Maps		✓														✓			✓
Coming Back to School		✓					✓						✓						✓
The Respiratory System		✓										✓						✓	
First Aid			✓	✓			✓											✓	✓
Consequences		✓																	
Solving Problems		✓																	✓
Climate		✓																✓	✓
Topography		✓					✓											✓	
Summer School		✓											✓		✓				
Keeping Track of Business		✓										✓	✓						✓
Throwing Tantrums	✓						✓			✓			✓						
The Distracting Influence	✓																		
Seven Chips	✓												✓		✓				
A Silent World	✓						✓						✓		✓				
Culture Shock	✓										✓							✓	
The Morning Routine	✓										✓								
The Marble Jar	✓												✓	✓					
The Reflection in the Window	✓												✓						
Studying French			✓		✓														✓
Pollution			✓	✓	✓			✓			✓								
Friends		✓						✓											
Alabama		✓						✓	✓			✓							
Houses and Boats										✓									
The Emergency Telephone Call	✓								✓	✓									
The Art Box	✓							✓	✓										
The Paycheck	✓		✓	✓															
Learning the Ropes	✓		✓		✓		✓	✓			✓							✓	✓
The Goldfish	✓		✓	✓															✓

	Motivation	Social Cog. Theory	Creativity	Affiliation	Anxiety	Learning/Perform. Goals	Attribution	Management	Instruction	Assessment	Male	Female
The Pearl										✓	✓	✓
Under the Bleachers											✓	✓
The Research Paper								✓		✓	✓	✓
Endangered Species										✓		✓
Horses and Aliens										✓	✓	
Proofreading								✓			✓	✓
The Stand-up Comic								✓			✓	
Halloween								✓	✓			✓
Letters								✓				✓
Cheerleading Tryouts	✓					✓	✓	✓				✓
The Perfectionist	✓			✓		✓	✓			✓		
Math Baseball	✓					✓	✓			✓		
Getting a Drink	✓			✓	✓			✓				✓
The Bulletin Board	✓	✓			✓	✓	✓				✓	
The Star Chart	✓									✓	✓	
The Concept Maps										✓		
Coming Back to School										✓	✓	
The Respiratory System								✓	✓			✓
First Aid								✓		✓		
Consequences								✓				✓
Solving Problems			✓					✓				✓
Climate								✓				✓
Topography	✓		✓									✓
Summer School		✓						✓				✓
Keeping Track of Business										✓		✓
Throwing Tantrums	✓											✓
The Distracting Influence			✓					✓				✓
Seven Chips								✓				✓
A Silent World								✓		✓		
Culture Shock										✓		
The Morning Routine										✓		✓
The Marble Jar								✓		✓		
The Reflection in the Window								✓				✓
Studying French						✓				✓		
Pollution		✓	✓							✓		
Friends												
Alabama				✓						✓		
Houses and Boats			✓							✓		✓
The Emergency Telephone Call								✓		✓		✓
The Art Box												✓
The Paycheck												✓
Learning the Ropes	✓							✓		✓		
The Goldfish												✓

CASE 1
The Goldfish

As the final school bell rings, most of the students in Ms. Bowman's first-grade class gather their belongings and hurry out the door. But Amy convinces her friend Lucy to linger for a few minutes while she checks on Ringo, the class's pet goldfish. As this week's "animal keeper" for the class, Amy has noticed that Ringo hasn't eaten any of his food for the past two days. In fact, all he does now is lie sideways on the surface of the water; he doesn't try to swim away anymore when she touches him. With her friend looking over her shoulder, Amy tries to give the fish a slight push towards a few flakes of food.

"He must be sleeping," she says. "Usually all I have to do is swish the water around to make him swim. He's acting really weird. Maybe he's *forgotten* how to eat and swim."

Lucy inspects the fish and then looks back at her friend, "I don't know, Amy. He's been sleeping an awful long time. He's not eating, either. I'll get Ms. Bowman, and maybe she can fix him."

Lucy hurries over to her teacher and grabs her by the hand. "Something's wrong," Amy declares as Lucy and Ms. Bowman approach the fish bowl. "He's not moving. He hasn't eaten for a long time."

When Ms. Bowman looks in the bowl, she realizes that Ringo has died. She delicately explains the situation and then wraps the fish in a paper towel. She assures the girls that she will give Ringo a proper burial as soon as she gets home.

Amy looks puzzled. "But...but...when my grandpa died last summer, he went away to heaven and didn't come back. Ringo's still here. If he's dead, he should be going to heaven."

"Do you want Ringo to go to heaven?" Amy nods, and her teacher smiles. "Well, then, I'll bet he'll go there just as soon as he possibly can."

As the two girls walk home, Lucy poses a question. "Do you have to eat in heaven?"

"I don't know," Amy responds. "I suppose so, or else you'd be hungry all the time."

"Oh, that makes sense." Lucy pauses for a moment, then asks, "Well, do you have to go potty in heaven?"

Amy rolls her eyes, indignantly puts her hands on her hips, and replies, "Of course not, silly! You know our Mommies and Ms. Bowman make us go potty before we go *anywhere*!"

"Oh, yeah, I forgot," laughs Lucy.

Possible questions for "The Goldfish":

1. *How can we interpret Amy's conclusions about eating and "going potty" from an information processing perspective?*

2.   *How can we interpret these conclusions from a Piagetian perspective?*

3.   *From a Piagetian perspective, how does the dead fish create disequilibrium for Amy?*

4.   *Preoperational egocentrism is the inability to see situations from someone else's perspective. Identify a possible instance of preoperational egocentrism in this case.*

5.   *How might taking care of pets in the classroom promote students' development?*

6.   *To what extent should Ms. Bowman have discussed the concepts of death and heaven with the entire class?*

CASE 2
Learning the Ropes

Today is Mindy's first day in Mr. Corbet's kindergarten class. Never before has she been in a room with so many other children her own age. She gets to sit at a blue table with two other girls and two boys. She has her very own chair, which is also blue; it even has her name taped on the back of it. Right now, she is coloring a name tag that will be taped to her place at the table, and she is chattering along with the other children who are sitting at the table with her.

"Hmmm...I think I'll color 'M' in pink," Mindy says. "I like pink. It's my favorite color."

Tanya, who is sitting next to her, says, "I think this letter is looking good. Oops, I colored outside the lines on the other one. Oh, well. What should I color the rest of my letters?"

"This is so easy," Jonathan pipes in. "I did this stuff last year when I went to preschool."

"I wonder if we're going to learn to read today," Grant muses.

The fifth member of the group, Tabitha, scans the room. "When did my Mommy leave?" she cries. A bit unnerved, she runs across the room to seek comfort from Mr. Corbet.

Pressing a little too hard, Mindy breaks a green crayon as she begins to color the letter *D* on her name tag. She looks around to see if anyone else has seen what she did; unfortunately, Jonathan has observed the mishap. She walks over to Mr. Corbet so that she can tell him she broke his crayon, but he's preoccupied with Tabitha and so sends her back to her seat. Mindy hides the broken crayon in a box and resumes coloring her name tag.

Jonathan raises his hand straight up in the air. Mindy looks up to see what he is trying to touch, but there's nothing there.

As Mr. Corbet approaches the blue table, Jonathan puts his hand back down. "Well, Jonathan," Mr. Corbet says loudly enough to attract the attention of the entire class, "where did you learn to raise your hand?"

"At preschool," Jonathan replies. He points to Mindy. "That girl broke your crayon."

Mr. Corbet squats down between Mindy and Jonathan. He gently covers Jonathan's hand with his own and curls the boy's pointed finger inward. "It's not nice to points at others or to tattle on them." Jonathan frowns and pulls his hand out of his teacher's grasp.

"What's your new friend's name?" Mr. Corbet asks, looking at Mindy.

Jonathan shrugs his shoulders. "I don't know."

Mr. Corbet smiles at Mindy and asks, "Would you like to tell him your name?"

Mindy looks at Mr. Corbet, then whispers, "Mindy. I...I didn't mean to break your crayon."

"It's okay, Mindy," Mr. Corbet reassures her. "Sometimes that happens with crayons when we press on them too hard. I know you didn't mean to break anything. It's not a big deal. In fact, the more practice you have using crayons, the less likely you will be to break them. So, then...let's find out who else is sitting at the blue table with Mindy and Jonathan...."

After the children have finished coloring their name tags, Mr. Corbet announces, "Okay, class, it's time to go to recess." Mindy isn't sure what this "recess" thing is, but she can tell by her classmates' excitement that it must be something good.

Mr. Corbet continues. "I'm going to have you line up at the outside door one table at a time. Hmmm...I see that the children at the red table are waiting very nicely. So, red table, you may be the first ones to line up. Please walk, *walk slowly and quietly*, to the outside door."

Two members of the red table run to be first in line. Ignoring them, Mr. Corbet says, "My, I like how Sam *walks* to the door. Did you see how he *walked*, class? It shows that he's definitely ready to be a kindergartner!"

Mr. Corbet next summons the yellow table. "Wow! Did you notice how everyone in the yellow group *walked*? I can tell that I have a smart class this year."

Mindy squirms in her seat until she hears her teacher call the blue table. When he does so, she makes a concerted effort to walk, not run, to join the line.

Once outside, Mindy stands near Mr. Corbet and watches the other children play on the playground equipment. She has finally concluded that *recess* must be a special place that has swings, monkey bars, tricycles, and other things to play on. A recess is like a park, she thinks, only smaller. Unlike her kindergarten classroom, recess is a place where running is allowed. Mindy runs to play with Tanya, her new friend from the blue table.

While the class is outside, Mr. Corbet sometimes blows a loud whistle at particular students. Mindy realizes that the sound of the whistle must not be a good thing, because the children he's whistled at have to stop what they're doing and talk with him, and they usually don't look too happy afterwards. Mindy wants to avoid the whistle at all costs, although she's not exactly sure how to go about doing that.

Mindy and Tanya spend most of their play time on the swings. At one point, a girl in a yellow dress pushes Tanya to the ground and then climbs on Tanya's swing as if nothing had happened. Tanya begins to cry, and Mindy looks around for Mr. Corbet. Seeing him close by, she raises her hand and waves it to get his attention.

As Mr. Corbet approaches the girls, Mindy starts to point at the girl in the yellow dress but then immediately closes her fist tight. She nods her head toward the guilty child. "See that girl in the yellow dress?" she asks her teacher. "Well, she pushed Tanya off the swings...."

Possible questions for "Learning the Ropes":

1. *Children don't always know what is expected of them when they first come to school. What evidence do we see that Mindy lacks knowledge about "how things are done" at school?*

2. *At the beginning of the case study, we see Mindy and Tanya talking while they color, yet they don't seem to be listening to each other. How would Piaget explain this event? How would Vygotsky explain it?*

3. *Children sometimes develop misunderstandings of what certain words mean. What meaning does Mindy construct for the concept "recess"? What information does she use in constructing this meaning?*

4. *What strategies does Mr. Corbet use to teach his students appropriate classroom behavior?*

5. *Vicarious reinforcement occurs when individuals increase the frequency of a response after they observe another person being reinforced for the same response. What evidence do we see that Mindy has experienced vicarious reinforcement?*

6. *Vicarious punishment occurs when individuals reduce the frequency of a response after they observe another person being punished for the same response. What evidence do we see that Mindy has experienced vicarious punishment?*

7. *What strategy does Mr. Corbet use to make his students feel at home in their new classroom?*

CASE 3
The Paycheck

Rodney, a boy in Ms. Tollefson's kindergarten class, has volunteered to stay after school to help clean up after a messy class art project. As he walks by Ms. Tollefson's desk, he notices her monthly paycheck lying beside her purse.

"Is that a check?" Rodney asks.

"Why, yes, it is," Ms. Tollefson replies, smiling.

"It looks just like the ones my mom and dad bring home all the time."

"Well, that's because your mom and dad both work for the city. I work for the city, too, so I get the same kind of check that they do."

Rodney is shocked, "You have a *job*??!!"

"Yes, of course," says Ms. Tollefson.

"Well, where do you work?"

"I work *here*. My job is teaching you children."

"You get paid for being here? I thought you were just here 'cause you love us."

"Well, I do love all of you. But I also get paid to work, just like your mom and dad get paid to work. Just like your parents, I need money to pay for things like food, medicine, and clothes."

"No, you don't. Teachers don't need money. When you're in this building you always get food from the cafeteria where we get our morning snacks, and you have clothes everyday 'cause you wear them. In fact, all you have to do is go over to that closet," he points to a small closet in the back of the room, "and grab a new outfit."

"Rodney, I keep my clothes at home just like you do."

"You have a home? I didn't know teachers left the building."

"You thought I *slept* here?"

"Well, actually I never thought about you sleeping. I just thought that this was your home."

"No. I sleep—live, actually—in a house just like you do. As a matter of fact, my house is just a few blocks from yours. You may even show up at my doorstep when you go trick-or-treating for Halloween tomorrow night."

"I think you're teasing me, Ms. Tollefson. Teachers don't live in houses. Teachers belong at school."

"Can't I be other things besides a teacher, Rodney? For example, did you know that I go skiing every weekend in the winter? So I'm a skier as well as a teacher. See, here's a picture of me skiing at Winter Park."

"You can't fool me, Ms. Tollefson," Rodney responds cheerfully as he skips out the door. "I know you're just a teacher."

"Happy Halloween!" yells Ms. Tollefson.

Rodney pokes his head back inside the classroom. "I knew it! You were trying to trick me 'cause it's Halloween!" Laughing, he runs down the hall before his teacher can reply.

Possible questions for "The Paycheck":

1.   From the perspective of Piaget's theory, what evidence of preoperational reasoning does Rodney exhibit?
2.   How might we explain Rodney's behavior from an information processing perspective?
3.   Transductive reasoning is making a mental leap from one specific thing to another, such as identifying one event as the cause of another simply because the two events occur close together in time. When did Rodney exhibit transductive reasoning?

CASE 4
The Art Box

Except for Lilly, who has suddenly lost her art box, all of Mr. King's third graders are in line and ready to go to Ms. Wilson's art class. Lilly checks her backpack but finds it empty. She doesn't remember taking her art supplies home, but she must have, because her markers, scissors, colored pencils, and glue are nowhere to be found. Finally giving up, Lilly runs to join her friends at the end of the line.

After she and her father have looked everywhere at home yet still have found no sign of the art box, Lilly tells Mr. King that her art supplies are missing. Mr. King mentions the situation to the class, suggests that maybe someone accidentally picked up the wrong box, and asks that all of the children look carefully inside their desks. None of the children finds either the box or its contents.

Over the weekend, Lilly and her father go shopping to replace the supplies she has lost. After arriving back home, Lilly's father painstakingly writes "Lilly" on each new item with a black, permanent marker. Yet by Thursday of the following week, Lilly cannot find the crayons and bottle of glue her father has recently purchased. She assures Mr. King that she has kept her supplies in her art box and that the box has remained in her desk the entire week. Mr. King doesn't know what to make of the situation but is beginning to think that Lilly is either very forgetful or very disorganized. And when Lilly's father has to buy yet another round of art supplies for his daughter, he is not at all pleased.

A few weeks later, Lilly sees Anne using a bottle of glue with the name "Lilly" written on it. Lilly confronts her classmate. "Where did you get that glue?"

"My mom bought it for me," Anne replies.

"Then how come it has my name written on it?" Lilly asks.

"'Cause my sister's name is Lilly and we share everything."

"I don't believe you. I'm tellin' the teacher."

After listening to Lilly's complaint, Mr. King confronts Anne. "Honey, where did you get that bottle of glue?"

"My mom gave it to me and my sister, Lilly."

"Are you sure?" asks Mr. King.

"Yes," Anne replies. "My mom always gives me things, 'cause she loves me."

"I see." Mr. King pauses, then adds, "I think it's time the two of you get back to work."

Suspecting that Anne is being dishonest, Mr. King sifts through the contents of Anne's desk while the class is at recess. He finds two art boxes with Lilly's name on them, several boxes of crayons marked with various children's initials, an assortment of glue bottles, and a "Colorado Rockies" pen in the shape of a baseball bat that he's pretty sure belongs to Owen. Leaving these items where he's found them, Mr. King calls Anne's parents and requests a conference immediately after school. Just before the final bell, Mr. King informs Anne that her parents are coming to pick her up and asks her to stay in her seat until they arrive.

"What's this about?" says Anne's father, Mr. Walker, as he ignores Mr. King's outstretched hand. "I had to cancel several clients at the office to come to this meeting."

"I'm delighted to finally meet you both," Mr. King responds. "I'm also grateful that you were able to come on such short notice. Perhaps we can sit at the reading table over here. I apologize for the size of the chairs. They're meant for six-year-olds rather than adults, I'm afraid."

Once Anne and her parents have taken their seats at the table, Mr. King continues. "This may seem like a strange question, but I would like to know if you have another daughter—one named Lilly."

"Lilly?" Ms. Walker seems puzzled. "No, Anne is our only child."

"You called me away from the office to ask if we have another *daughter*?" Mr. Walker asks angrily.

Mr. King tries to keep his composure. "Well, over the past few weeks, a number of my students have found items missing from their desks. This afternoon, I found most of them in Anne's desk." He pauses to see if either Anne or one of her parents has anything to say at this point, but all three are silent. "I can't seem to get a straight answer from Anne as to how other children's things have ended up in her desk. I was hoping that maybe...if we could get together to talk about it...we could figure out what's going on."

Mr. Walker stands up, clearly uncomfortable with Mr. King's implied accusation. He turns to his daughter and says, "Okay, Anne, let's go take a look at your desk." Anne leads the way, and the three adults follow. When Anne opens her desk, several items marked "Lilly" are lying in plain sight.

Mr. Walker is obviously taken aback at the discovery. "So how'd these things get in your desk, Anne?" he asks.

"Kids gave them to me so I'd be their friend," Anne replies tentatively as she looks down at the floor.

Mr. Walker turns to Mr. King. "There you have it, Mr. King. My daughter knows I expect her to obey rules like not stealing and lying. Don't you, Anne?" When Anne nods in agreement, he continues, "If she says the other kids gave them to her, then they *gave* them to her."

Mr. King looks Anne directly in the eye. "Anne, didn't you tell me these things belonged to your sister Lilly?"

"Like my wife said earlier, Anne doesn't have a sister Lilly!" Mr. Walker barks.

Mr. King is firm. "Tell your parents what you told me earlier, Anne."

"I said my *friend*, Lilly, gave me her art boxes and some of her crayons and glue. You just didn't listen, Mr. King."

"Hmmm...," Mr. King responds pensively. "I think...."

Mr. Walker rudely interrupts. "She says she didn't take that stuff. It's not her fault that she's so popular. She obeys me at home—no stealing and no lying. Why should she be different in school? Sure, sometimes she's a little brat, but what kid isn't?" Mr. Walker speaks as if Anne weren't even in the room.

Ms. Walker reaches out and pulls her daughter toward her in a protective embrace. "She's just a little girl. What if she did take that stuff...?"

"She didn't!" screams Mr. Walker.

"It's just some crayons and pencils. Altogether it can't be worth more than five dollars," Ms. Walker suggests. "Why should she be punished if none of the items was destroyed?"

"I'm afraid that you both are missing the point here," Mr. King responds. "Lilly, one of the other children in my class, has had to replace her art supplies twice now because they've suddenly disappeared, and then today I find Lilly's possessions in Anne's desk."

"How do you know Lilly didn't just give these things to Anne?!" demands Mr. Walker.

"Well, for one thing, several weeks ago Lilly told me that her art box was missing. It seems unlikely that she would tell me that if she knew she had given it to Anne."

Mr. Walker responds angrily. "So you're taking *her* word over my daughter's? I expect Anne to follow my rules, and I think she does. How do we know that Lilly isn't lying? Where are *her* parents? Why isn't she being called on the carpet the way Anne is right now?"

"But look at the evidence in her desk. The items are clearly labeled with other children's names. Anne can't possibly be completely innocent...."

"Leave my daughter out of this!" Mr. Walker screams. "I expect you to set an example for my child. You should have had all of the facts before you went accusing someone of such a horrible crime. Come on, Anne, let's go home. Mr. King needs to think about what he has done!" Mr. King watches in total frustration as the Walkers leave his classroom in a huff.

NOTE: Throughout her school career, Anne continued to take no responsibility for her actions, nor were her parents ever willing to admit their daughter's wrongdoings.

Possible questions for "The Art Box":

1. *From the perspective of Kohlberg's theory of moral development, how might you characterize Anne's behavior?*

2. *Researchers such as Baumrind (1971) and Maccoby and Martin (1983) believe that parents display different styles (i.e., authoritative, authoritarian, permissive, and uninvolved) for rearing their children. What type of parenting style does Mr. Walker exhibit?*

3. *What type of parenting style does Ms. Walker exhibit?*

4. *Mr. King makes a common mistake: His first contact with the Walkers is a negative one. As a teacher, how might you initiate more positive initial contacts with your students' parents?*
5. *Why do you think Anne stole the items?*
6. *In all likelihood, since Anne was reinforced for stealing, she will steal again. As the teacher, what can you do to prevent another theft from occurring again in your classroom?*

CASE 5
The Emergency Telephone Call

Near the end of the school day, Mr. Wadsworth has an emergency telephone call and finds that he must leave his fifth-grade class temporarily unattended. He puts Sandy, a particularly trustworthy student, in charge, asking her to keep the other students in their seats and on task. He also asks her to report any misbehaviors to him upon his return.

After listening to their teacher's footsteps grow fainter and fainter as he walks down the hall, many of the children begin talking and joking with one another. The longer Mr. Wadsworth is gone, the louder the volume of their chatter becomes. "Oh, great!" thinks Sandy. "Do I report *all* of them?"

Suzanne, a girl whom Sandy admires, shouts, "Hey, let's play some tricks on Mr. Wadsworth!" She runs up to her teacher's desk, grabs several tacks from the desk drawer, and strategically scatters them on Mr. Wadsworth's chair at the reading table. Sandy approaches her friend and whispers, "Suzanne, you need to put those tacks back. You know this is wrong. Mr. Wadsworth might hurt himself."

"Lighten up, Sandy. Besides, he'll never know who did it, will he?"

"It's wrong...."

"It's only wrong if you get *caught*, Sandy."

Suzanne sees a bottle of glue on Mr. Wadsworth's desk. Ignoring Sandy's pleas to stop, she takes several of the textbooks lying on Mr. Wadsworth's desk and glues some of the pages together. Then, hiding the empty glue bottle in her desk, Suzanne looks around to see if any of the other children have noticed what she has done, but they seem to be wrapped up in off-task activities of their own.

After pausing to think about additional pranks that she can play, Suzanne puts the class hamster, George, in the bottom file drawer of her teacher's desk. As an afterthought, she pours some water in a plastic cup and places it in the drawer along with the hamster.

"Suzanne, what you're doing isn't nice to George, to Mr. Wadsworth, or to me. Mr. Wadsworth is going to be really angry at me for letting you do these things. I know you think you're being funny, but you're not!"

"Sandy, I thought we were friends."

"We are."

"Friends trust one another and share secrets. Anyway, there won't be a problem if I don't get caught."

"Well, yeah, but I don't like keeping this kind of secret. Mr. Wadsworth trusts me. Besides, he'll probably punish the whole class for what you've done."

Ignoring Sandy, Suzanne grabs red and black permanent markers and proceeds to draw pictures of Mr. Wadsworth on the dry eraser board hanging on the wall. The class grows quiet as they watch Suzanne draw her pictures. Sandy lays her head on her desk in hopeless resignation.

"Suzanne, those are permanent markers," Dillon calls out. "You won't be able to erase that stuff."

"Oh, come on, Wadsworth can get rid of them," Suzanne retorts. "All he has to do is use rubbing alcohol and the ink will come right off."

"Why should *he* clean up *your* mess?" Molly asks indignantly.

"Man, you're really gonna get in trouble!" Blake warns.

Suzanne turns and glares at her classmates. "I won't get in trouble unless there's a 'narc' in here."

The others look to Sandy for help, but she still has her head on her desk. When the final bell rings and Mr. Wadsworth has still not returned to his classroom, the children slowly gather their things and leave for home.

Suzanne leaves the uncapped markers on the eraser board shelf and gathers her belongings. "Do you want to walk home together?" she asks Sandy.

"No, I...uh...have to stay after school for choir."

"Oh, I see. You're going to 'narc' on me, aren't you?"

"Uh, no, probably not. No, of course not. But I think you should tell Mr. Wadsworth what you've done."

"Oh, come on, Sandy. It was all just a joke."

"Well, it wasn't a very funny one."

After Suzanne leaves, Sandy walks to the office and asks Ms. Leary, the school secretary, for some rubbing alcohol.

"Why do you need it?" Ms. Leary asks her.

"Uh...well, you see...uh...someone accidentally got some permanent marker on the erasable marker board. I was going to clean it off for Mr. Wadsworth." Sandy looks down at her feet.

"Honey, you don't have to worry about it," Ms. Leary tells her. "Mr. Schroeder, the custodian, will clean it up."

"That's okay, I don't mind. I...uh...kinda like cleaning the boards."

"No, that's Mr. Schroeder's job. You run on home."

Sandy returns to her classroom to wait for Mr. Wadsworth's return. She should have been home a half an hour ago. "Great," she thinks, "now Mom is going to be mad at me, too."

Mr. Wadsworth walks into the room, "Sandy, your mother just called. She's very worried about you. Why are you still here?"

Before she can respond, Mr. Wadsworth sees the board. "What the heck...who wrote on the board with permanent markers?"

Sandy bursts into tears. "I tried to make them behave. Really I did!"

"The *whole class* did this?"

"No, just someone...just one person. But no one did anything about it, so I didn't, either."

Mr. Wadsworth stoops down to Sandy's level, looks her straight in the eye, and asks, "Who did this, Sandy?"

She shrugs her shoulders.

"If you don't tell me who was responsible for this mess, then you will have to be the one to clean it up."

Sandy stares at the floor.

Mr. Wadsworth leaves the room, returning shortly with a bottle of clear liquid. He hands the bottle to Sandy, "I expected better of you, Sandy. Maybe cleaning the marker board will refresh your memory. By the way, your mother is on her way over."

While Sandy cleans the board, Mr. Wadsworth sits at his desk to grade papers. He opens the bottom drawer to look for his grading book, only to find the class hamster scampering about and water sloshing from one side of the drawer to the other. He sees, too, that all the teaching materials he keeps in that drawer have been chewed by the hamster and saturated with water.

Mr. Wadsworth explodes. "Sandy, George is in my desk! He's ruined everything. Who did this? Tell me *now*!"

Sandy replies so quietly that Mr. Wadsworth can barely hear her. "She did more stuff, too. She ruined some of your books. She...uh...glued a bunch of pages together."

Gathering his composure, Mr. Wadsworth repeats his question. "Who did this, Sandy?"

"Suzanne. She said I'd be a narc if I told. Please don't tell her I told you, Mr. Wadsworth. *Please!*"

NOTE: Suzanne was officially charged with a misdemeanor: She was suspended three days for willful destruction of school property. The municipal court judge mandated that before she could return to school, her parents would have to reimburse the school district for the damages she had caused. Several years after the incident, Suzanne and Sandy still weren't speaking to each other.

Possible questions for "The Emergency Telephone Call":

1. *From Kohlberg's perspective, in what stage of moral development is each of the girls?*
2. *Is it appropriate for Mr. Wadsworth to put Sandy in charge of the class during his absence? Why or why not?*
3. *Do you think the entire class should be punished for allowing Suzanne to vandalize the classroom? Why or why not?*

CASE 6
Houses and Boats

While waiting for a visit from the local fire chief, Mr. Rodriguez asks his third graders to draw floor plans of their homes—as he puts it, to "draw what a bird would see if the roof were missing." Once the fire chief arrives, the children will use red colored markers to create several fire exit routes in their floor plans.

As the children work at tables of four students each, Mr. Rodriguez walks around the room to oversee their efforts. He notices that Jenny is copying Tian's floor plan on her own paper.

"Jenny, do you live in the same house as Tian?" he asks her.

"No."

"Then why are you copying his drawing?"

"Because I don't know how to draw things on my own."

"Of course you do. I'm asking you to draw *your* house, not just any old house."

"I can't."

"Jenny, I was your kindergarten teacher. I remember that you used to draw *lovely* pictures."

"Maybe, but I don't remember how to draw houses anymore."

"You don't *remember* how to draw them?"

"That's right. I can't do it by myself, so you'll have to show me how."

"Well, I can get you started, anyway. How many stories does your house have?"

"Two."

"Okay. Let's start with the first floor. How many rooms are there on the first floor of your house?"

"Uh...let's see...there's the living room and the dining room and the kitchen and the bathroom. That's four."

"Is there also a hallway with stairs going up to the second floor?"

"Yes."

"Okay. Now what shape is your house? What shape would it be if a bird were looking down at it?"

"A rectangle, I guess."

"So start by drawing a rectangle on your paper. Good, now why don't you show me where the front door is in this rectangle house of yours, and then we can talk about where each room should go and where we should put the stairs...."

During the fire chief's visit, Ms. Piesman, the art teacher, arrives carrying a stack of watercolor paintings. "Say, your students did a wonderful job painting these boats," she tells Mr. Rodriguez. "I thought I'd hang them up in the hallway. Would that be all right with you?"

"Sounds like a great idea! If you have time now, I can help you hang them."

"Thanks, I'd appreciate that."

As the two teachers begin hanging the paintings in the hallway on both sides of the classroom door, Mr. Rodriguez comments, "This is the first time all year that I've had a chance to see any of the children's art work." He pauses to stare at the paintings. "Hey! All of these boats look the same."

"Of course."

"I mean, everyone used the exact same proportions, the same colors, the same...everything!"

"Yes," Ms. Piesman sighs. "It took me awhile, but I finally got everyone to think on the same wavelength."

Possible questions for "Houses and Boats":

1.   From Erik Erikson's perspective, in what stage of development is Jenny?
2.   Why might Jenny be having trouble creating her floor plan?
3.   Is it wise for Ms. Piesman to insist that the children all make their boats in the same way? Why or why not?

CASE 7
Alabama

Until last week, Tom attended a small school in Alabama at which almost everyone, teachers and students alike, were people he'd known for years. But now that his family has moved to Indiana, he has enrolled at a junior high school with more than 300 students in just the seventh and eighth grades alone. Naturally, he doesn't know a soul.

On his first day at his new school, Tom is dumbfounded by the other students' language. They talk a lot faster than the people in Alabama do, and no one addresses teachers as "ma'am" or "sir." The students dress differently, too. Most of them wear oversized T-shirts and ripped jeans, and some of the boys wear their pants so low on their hips that their boxer shorts show. Amazingly, none of the teachers seems to mind how the kids are dressed. Back in Alabama, Tom would have been sent home for such attire.

In his first-period English class, Tom notices several of his classmates snickering at his white shirt, necktie, and khaki pants. One of them, a boy named Sam, inquires, "Hey, man, where you from?"

"Alabama," Tom replies. "This is my first day here."

"Don't you wear jeans in Allaaabaaamma?" Sam asks him, stretching out "Alabama" to mimic Tom's southern drawl.

"Of course we wear jeans," Tom responds. "But I wouldn't dream of coming to school with holes in my pants or with my underwear showing."

Sam winks at the small group of girls who are watching the interaction. "I bet you wouldn't, Allaaabaaamma." Tom hears the girls snicker and feels his face turn red. He buries his face in the textbook his teacher has just given him.

Tom stays after school to try out for the boys' track team, a team on which he excelled back in Alabama. Sam and several of the other boys in his English class are at the tryouts as well. Tom is the only one wearing a bright red lycra jogging suit. Everyone else is wearing blue cotton sweat pants and white T-shirts. Tom realizes that blue and white must be the school colors.

"What's the matter, Alabama, don't they have sweat pants where you come from?" Sam jeers. "Who do you think you are—Michael Jordan? Say, Allaaabaaamma, I sure hope you don't run as slow as you talk."

Several of the other boys are trembling with laughter. Tom says nothing, but he grits his teeth and clenches his fists in anger as he walks over to the bleachers to sit near the track coach, Mr. Davis. He wishes his family had never moved to Indiana. The students are so strange here, and he feels completely out of place.

"Okay, gentlemen, let's get started," Coach Davis calls out. As all the boys gather around him, he continues, "There are more than 60 of you here today. I'm very pleased that so many of you have come out. Unfortunately, I only have 24 spots on the team, so we'll have to see which of you are the fastest. I'm going to divide you into groups of three and have you race around the track. We'll see who's the fastest in each group."

Tom finds himself in the same group as Sam and a boy named Eddie, who's in his science class. As the three boys run around the track, they are initially neck and neck. But suddenly Eddie trips, knocking Sam, and the two boys fall. Tom looks back and sees both Sam and Eddie lying on the track. Sam seems to have gotten a nasty gash on his knee. Tom immediately turns around and trots over to Sam, grabs his hand, and helps him get up.

Coach Davis approaches the threesome to make sure everyone is all right. "It looks like we'll have to run this race again," Tom tells him.

"Hey, Alabama," Sam says, but he doesn't mock Tom this time. "Why didn't you finish the race? You could easily have won it."

"When I win, I want to know that it's a 'true' win."

A short time later, Sam and Eddie both outrun Tom, and Tom is eliminated from further consideration. Sam offers his hand to Tom. "Good try, Alabama. Thanks for letting me have another go at it." Tom shakes Sam's hand and smiles, trying to hide his disappointment about not making the team.

The following morning, many of the boys in Tom's English class are reveling in their success at making the track team. In an attempt to draw attention to themselves, several of them start to pick on Tom.

"Hey, Alabama, don't you know your way around a track?" David taunts. "Or maybe a circle's just too much for you!"

"Did your Mommy comfort you when she found out you're a loser, Alabama?" Greg adds.

"Wow, Alabama, you're wearing your shirt untucked today," Mick observes. "Aren't *you* a cool dude!"

"Why don't you guys just leave Alabama alone?" Sam suggests, obviously annoyed.

"What's with you, Sam?" David asks him. "Maybe you're from Alabama, too, and you're just hiding your accent."

"No, I'm not from Alabama!" Sam exclaims. He lowers his voice and continues, "Anyway, what if I was? Nothing's wrong with comin' from there."

At the end of class, Sam slips Tom a note. It reads: "There's a computer club meeting tonight. None of these boys are in it. Call me."

NOTE: At Tom's school in Alabama, there had been no competition for extracurricular activities; the school was so small that clubs and sports teams typically accepted anyone who wanted to join them. Tom openly expressed his feelings of discomfort regarding the more competitive atmosphere of his new school. Aside from the computer club, he didn't participate in extracurricular activities.

Possible questions for "Alabama":

1. *Characterize Tom's initial reaction to his new school.*
2. *How successfully does Tom adjust to the "culture" of his new school?*
3. *In which of Kohlberg's stages of moral development does Tom appear to be?*
4. *Many junior high schools have a "no cuts" policy with regard to extracurricular activities; in other words, teams and clubs accept anyone who wants to join them. Do you think that this is a good idea? Why or why not?*
5. *It is not unusual for students at this age to make jokes at someone else's expense. As a teacher, what should you do if you hear such teasing in your classroom?*
6. *As a teacher, how might you help Tom make friends at his new school?*

CASE 8
Friends

Tanner and Ethan have been Jared's closest friends since preschool. The three boys have always had much in common; over the years, they've had similar interests —first in Legos, then in lizards, and eventually in model trains. They belonged to the same Cub Scout troop, and they've always made sure they were on the same team in the city baseball and basketball leagues. They've even dressed alike, wearing T-shirts, jeans, high-top sneakers, and Atlanta Braves baseball caps. At their small neighborhood school, they've always been in the same class.

But now that they're in junior high school, things seem to be different. Although Jared and Ethan have lockers next to each other, the three boys have been assigned to different homerooms and different classes, and each one eats during a different lunch period, so they hardly ever see one another during the school day. Furthermore, Tanner and Ethan don't seem to be the same guys that they used to be. Tanner started wearing an earring the week after school began. His clothes are different, too. His baggy pants hang down low on his hips, and his shirts are always so large that they reach to his knees. He's usually so interested in flirting with girls in the hallway or riding his new skateboard with the other "skaters" in the school parking lot that he has little time for Jared.

Ethan has changed, too, although in different ways than Tanner has. For example, he's about six inches taller than he was last year. His voice has grown deep like his dad's. He's become a real "neatnik," with his hair carefully combed and his designer shirts tucked carefully inside his well-pressed pants. He's joined the soccer team and stays for two hours of soccer practice every day after school. Like Tanner, Ethan seems to have little interest in maintaining his friendship with Jared.

Thinking that he would be too busy playing football after school with his friends, Jared didn't sign up for any of the extracurricular activities at his new school. So he comes home right after school each day and retreats to the basement to play with his model trains.

"Gosh, Jared, I haven't seen Ethan and Tanner over here for quite some time," his mother comments one day. "Don't you ever see them at school?"

"Not really, Mom," Jared replies. "And they're usually too busy when I ask them to come over."

"Well, you know, I ran into Ethan's mother at the grocery store the other day, and she said that Ethan made lots of new friends when he joined the soccer team. Maybe you should think about joining one of the teams or clubs at school, too. What about the swimming team, or the Spanish Club, or maybe the school band?"

As luck would have it, Jared sees announcements for school band tryouts posted around the school building the following day. Having taken a few trumpet lessons when he was in fourth grade, Jared thinks that playing trumpet in the band might be fun. When he gets home that afternoon, he pulls his trumpet out of his closet and begins to practice. "It's coming back to me," he happily discovers.

Possible questions for "Friends":

1. *The transition to junior high school is often an unsettling time for students because many changes seem to occur almost simultaneously. What specific changes do we see at this point in time?*
2. *If you were a junior high school teacher, what strategies might you use to make new students feel more comfortable and secure?*
3. *Explain Jared's newly found interest in extracurricular activities from the perspective of social cognitive theory.*

CASE 9
Pollution

Like most of her classmates at Central High, 14-year-old Laura wears the same attire to school every day: stone-washed jeans with torn knees, an oversized T-shirt, and hiking boots. Her first stop when she arrives at school in the morning is the restroom, where she recurls her hair and touches up her makeup. She usually lingers for 10 or 15 minutes so that she can share the latest school gossip with her friends.

Laura's extended restroom visits often make her late for her first-hour study hall. When Ms. Watkins, the school counselor, chastises her for her consistent tardiness, Laura replies, "Everyone will notice if I don't look my absolute *best*. I don't want people to think I'm a geek!"

"Do you *like* people looking at you, Laura?" Ms. Watkins asks.

"Well, sure. I mean, everybody does, don't you think?"

Ms. Watkins smiles. "Yes, Laura, I think that almost everybody likes to have attention once in a while. Maybe that's just part of being human. And I know a class where you can be the center of attention—a class in which everyone wants to hear your opinion about things. Let's see if we can find a place for you in Mr. Marculescu's Debating I class. It meets first hour, the same time as your study hall. There's a catch, though. If you're late, then you won't have a chance to participate in any debates."

"No problem, Ms. Watkins. For something like that, I can certainly be on time if I need to."

The following morning, Mr. Marculescu begins class by saying, "Today we're going to practice one of the topics that we'll be debating next week with South High School's Debating I class. The topic is this: How do we solve the nation's pollution problems? We'll begin by having several of you get up in front of the class, one at a time, to present your ideas about how to deal with pollution. I'll pretend that I'm someone from the South High team and challenge each of you. Who would like to be our first volunteer?"

Not realizing what she might be getting herself into, Laura eagerly raises her hand.

"Okay, Laura, you want to give it a shot? Come on up here and stand behind the podium on the right. I'll take the podium on the left."

"Can't I just stay here in my seat?"

"I'd prefer that you stand up here where everyone can see you and hear what you're saying."

As Laura approaches the front of the room, she begins to have second thoughts about joining this class. She decides to put up a good front by pretending that she knows what she's doing. She stands behind her assigned podium with the best air of confidence she can muster.

From behind his own podium, Mr. Marculescu addresses the rest of the class. "Just a reminder about what the rest of you need to do here. As Laura presents her position regarding how we might solve the country's pollution problems, you should all be listening carefully for flaws in her arguments. Okay, Laura, go ahead and begin."

Laura hesitates as she looks around the room. "I...uh...I'm not sure I know what to say about this."

"Why don't you begin by talking about what you think the *causes* of pollution are?" Mr. Marculescu suggests. "I'm sure you have some good ideas, and we'd all like to hear them."

"You mean that you actually *care* what I say?" Laura asks.

"Of course," her teacher assures her. "What you have to say is *definitely* important." Mr. Marculescu looks pointedly at her, waiting for her to begin.

She swallows, then says, "Well, I think the government shouldn't allow people to sell gasoline. That way, we wouldn't have any more air pollution from car exhaust or other machines."

"You mean, people shouldn't be able to sell gasoline to *anyone*?" Mr. Marculescu queries. "Not even the mail carriers, the garbage collectors, the school bus drivers?"

"Right. People could take their garbage to the landfills as they walk to work. Some of them could run or ride bikes. Most people in the United States are too fat anyway, so the exercise would do them good."

"How much time do you think it would take a single mother with an infant and a child in elementary school to get to her job if she had to stop at a daycare center, an elementary school, and a landfill on her way every day?"

"Oh, not too long. She could just put her kids in a covered bike carrier and throw the garbage bag on top of it. Besides, she wouldn't have to go to the landfill *every* day, only when the trash piles up."

"But while the trash is piling up at home, won't it attract mice and rats?"

"Well, then I guess she would just have to go the landfill more often."

"But what if her job is miles away from her house?"

"She should move, of course!"

"What about the elderly? How would they get their trash to the landfills?"

"They'd have their children or neighbors do it for them."

"But wouldn't the landfill itself cause some pollution?"

"Not really, because we could just have some scientist pour chemicals over it until it dissolves."

"Wouldn't the chemicals pollute our air and water?"

"Science is changing every day, and scientists are always learning new things. Maybe someone could find a new chemical that would get rid of all the bad things. It's possible, you know."

Mr. Marculescu continues to challenge Laura's reasoning, but the girl remains firmly convinced that her proposed ban on gasoline sales is a viable solution to the country's pollution problems, and she finds Mr. Marculescu's questions more annoying than enlightening. As she puts it so succinctly to her friends while restyling her hair in the restroom later that day, "Mr. Marculescu can be so *unreasonable!*"

Possible questions for "Pollution":

1. *From a developmental standpoint, how might we explain Laura's preoccupation with her appearance?*
2. *From Piaget's perspective, in which stage of cognitive development is Laura?*
3. *According to Piaget, egocentrism is an inability to see things from another person's perspective. What evidence do we see of formal operational egocentrism in Laura's reasoning?*
4. *How is Laura's reasoning affected by what she does and doesn't know about pollution?*
5. *According to Piaget, disequilibrium is the state of being unable to explain new events in terms of existing schemas. How does Mr. Marculescu create disequilibrium for Laura?*
6. *In what ways might a debating class contribute to students' cognitive, linguistic, and moral development?*

CASE 10
Studying French

Every Thursday night of her freshman year, Karen studies for the quiz she knows she will have in her French I class the following morning. She begins her study sessions by preparing flash cards for the week's vocabulary words, writing each new word on one side of an index card and then copying the word's definition onto the flip side. After completing her flash cards, Karen locks herself in her room, turns on the radio, then repeats each word and its definition five times to herself. Unfortunately, her strategy doesn't seem to be working very well. Although she's getting *A's* and *B's* in her other classes, the highest score she's earned in French I is a 72%— *C*-.

In May, as she and her friends are signing up for next year's classes, Karen is trying to decide whether or not to take a second year of French. She is well aware that the college she wants to attend requires its students to have at least two years of a foreign language. And her two best friends, Dawnece and Claire, are urging her to take Mr. Lanier's third-hour French II class with them. Dawnece reminds her that the French club is going to Paris the following summer. "Besides," Dawnece says, "Mr. Lanier is so *cute*!"

Karen grins sheepishly. "Oh, what the heck! I can't possibly do any worse in French II than I've been doing in French I."

The following September, Karen begins to panic as the first test approaches in her French II class. "No matter how hard I try, I'm just no good at French," she thinks. "Will Dawnece think I'm stupid if I ask her to study with me? Claire probably doesn't study at all. She's lucky; her parents are both French, so she was *born* knowing this stuff."

Karen brings up the subject at lunch. "You know, our first French test is tomorrow."

"Yeah, what a pain," Dawnece replies. "I hate studying."

"Me, too," agrees Claire.

"Uh...yeah," Karen says. "Say, I was wondering if...uh...Dawnece, I thought maybe we could study together." She nervously scrutinizes Dawnece's facial expression, wondering if her friend will think she's crazy for asking.

But Dawnece apparently doesn't think she's crazy at all. "Hey, sure! Claire and I are going to study at my house at 6:30 tonight. Come join us."

Karen seems quite surprised. "You and *Claire*? Claire, you *study* for your French tests?"

Claire laughs. "Of course!"

"But your parents are *French*!"

"My mom moved to the United States when she was three, and my dad moved here when he was a teenager. You know perfectly well that both my parents speak English at home. My mom says she doesn't even *remember* any French. Besides, don't *you* study for your *English* tests?"

"Well, yeah, I *guess* so, but...."

"Like, it's the same thing!"

To prepare for her study session with Dawnece and Claire, Karen makes flash cards for all the vocabulary words the class has studied so far. She wonders whether her friends have completed their cards already or will make them while they study, instead. She spends an hour or so repeating the words and definitions on her flash cards and then arrives at Dawnece's door around 6:45.

"We started without you," Dawnece tells her. "I hope you don't mind."

When Karen notices that neither girl has any flash cards in front of her, she keeps her own cards buried at the bottom of her backpack. The study session continues where it left off.

"So, Dawnece," Claire asks, "what did you do for *attendre*?"

"Well, since *attendre* means 'to wait,' I came up with, 'Each time I *attend* something, I have to *wait* in line before I get in'."

"I came up with 'I can't *wait* to *attendre* in the driver's license line.' I think I like yours better."

Claire writes Dawnece's sentence in her notebook, and Karen decides to do likewise in her own notes. Even though Karen had gone through her flashcards less than an hour ago, she didn't remember what *attendre* means.

"Karen, what's your sentence for *attendre*?" Claire asks.

Naturally, Karen doesn't have a sentence at all, but she tries to save face. "Umm...mine's pretty much like Dawnece's."

"Okay," Dawnece says, "the next word is *demander*, which means 'to request'."

"Oh, I have a great one for that," Claire says. "My mom's *requests* are more like *demander* or *demands*."

"Good one!" Dawnece exclaims. She and Karen both write the sentence in their notebooks.

"Okay, the next word is *l'histoire*, which means 'story'," Claire says. "How about, *l'histoire* or *history* is a *story* about the world?"

"That should be easy enough to remember," agrees Dawnece.

"Is this how you guys always study?" Karen asks. "Like, making up sentences for each new word?"

"Sure," Dawnece answers.

"First we put the word in an English sentence, and then we put it in a French sentence," Claire adds. "For *l'histoire*, we might say, *a ce que dit l'histoire*, which means 'as the story goes...'."

"Wow!" says Karen. "What a good idea!"

Karen is nervous as Mr. Lanier passes out the French test, but she's determined to do well. "Okay, Karen, you can do this," she tells herself. She takes a deep breath and then looks at her test. "Okay, the first word is *l'histoire*. Let's see, 'history is a story about the world,' so *l'histoire* means 'story'. Okay, the second word is *demander*. Oh, yeah, 'my mom's requests are more like demands', so *demander* means 'to request'. Hey, I *know* this stuff. I really know it!"

Karen quickly finishes the vocabulary portion of the test and then breezes through her translation of the assigned excerpt from *Candide*. She finishes the test in thirty-five minutes, several minutes before most of her classmates.

The following Monday, Mr. Lanier returns the graded test papers. On Karen's paper, he's written "Good job!" across the top. On the back page of the test is an A—in bright red ink. She's answered all of her vocabulary words correctly, and she's made only a few minor mistakes in her translation of the excerpt from *Candide*.

Possible questions for "Studying French":

1. *Attribution is an individual's causal explanation for something that happens to an individual (e.g., success or failure experience). To what does Karen attribute Claire's success in French?*
2. *From an information processing perspective, characterize Karen's approach to studying French prior to her study session with her friends.*
3. *Characterize how Dawnece's and Claire's approach to studying French helps them encode and retrieve information from their long-term memory.*
4. *As a teacher, what things might you do to help students develop effective study strategies?*

CASE 11
The Reflection in the Window

Eight-year-old Jason seems to be staring out the window of his second-grade classroom. "Jason," Ms. Brown whispers, "you need to get back to the story you're writing with your spelling words." He nods, looks at the clock, then writes one more sentence on the paper in front of him. Within minutes, he is gazing out the window again. Ms. Brown sighs when she sees him off-task once again. She walks over to him and asks, "Do you think you need to move closer to my desk, where there won't be any windows to distract you?"

"Maybe that would be a good idea," Jason whispers.

Jason's response surprises Ms. Brown. She had expected that her threat would entice him to finish his work. But instead, she now has to follow through with the threat and find a place for him at the front of the room.

Midway through the morning, as his classmates enjoy recess outside, Jason remains in the classroom to work on assignments that he could easily have completed before recess began. While he works at a table at the back of the room, Ms. Brown moves his desk so that it is just a few feet away from her own.

"Jason, this is the fourth time in a row that you've missed out on morning recess, yet every day you spend even more time looking out the window than you did the day before. These consequences—missing recess and sitting next to me—are the only things that I can think of to get you back on track."

"Oh, I don't mind, Ms. Brown. I'd rather be sitting near you than looking at your reflection in the window." He is grinning from ear to ear.

Ms. Brown is both stunned and flattered. After thinking for a moment, she approaches Jason, stoops down to look him in the eye, and asks, "Why have you been staring at me?"

"'Cause you're beautiful. I like to watch you."

"Oh, I see.... Tell me, Jason, have you been staying in from recess on purpose?"

Jason looks down at his feet. "Yes," he whispers. "I love you, and it's the only time I get you all by myself." He then looks up at his teacher and asks, "Will you marry me, Ms. Brown...I mean, when I get big and everything?"

Ms. Brown smiles. "Jason, I would love to marry someone like you, but you see, I'm just not ready to get married."

"So when do you think you'll be ready?"

"Well, I'll tell you what—if you still want to marry me when you get big—bigger than me and old enough to grow a mustache—then we'll discuss it. Okay?"

He smiles. "You know, I *will* marry you. I won't change my mind about that."

"Jason, you will always hold a special place in my heart. In the meantime, I like for my guys to fulfill their responsibilities. One of *your* responsibilities is to do your work when I assign it. Okay?" Jason nods. "I wonder if we can think of another time—besides recess, I mean—when you and I could spend a little time together each day."

"Just me and you?" Jason asks.

Ms. Brown nods yes, then suggests, "How about if you become my morning helper since your mom drives you to school every day, and most of the time, you're here at least 15 minutes before the first bell rings? Maybe you could help me get things ready in the classroom before school starts."

"Wow, that would be great! Can I start tomorrow, Ms. Brown?"

"Sure, if it's okay with your mom. How about if I call her this afternoon?"

Jason's eyes light up, and he nods his head in enthusiastic agreement.

"But," Ms. Brown says, "there's just one little catch, Jason. I will let you be my morning helper *only* if you finish your work on time so that you can go to recess with the other children."

Jason offers his hand and replies, "It's a deal. Let's shake on it to make it official."

NOTE: After three weeks of being "morning helper," Jason decided that it was more fun playing ball with his peers on the playground before school started than spending time with his teacher.

Possible questions for "The Reflection in the Window":

1. *Use a behaviorist perspective to explain why Jason isn't getting his work done.*
2. *Ms. Brown makes at least two mistakes when she threatens to move Jason's desk near her own. What are they?*
3. *Is it appropriate for Ms. Brown to give Jason extra attention each morning before school starts? Why or why not?*
4. *It isn't at all unusual for students to develop crushes on their teachers. What might you do if one of your students develops a crush on you?*

CASE 12
The Marble Jar[1]

Of the 28 students in Mr. Fenwick's second-grade class, nine come from homes in which a language other than English is spoken. These students, plus four others who have been diagnosed as having learning disabilities, are reading at a preprimer (i.e., kindergarten) level or not at all, and many of them have not yet learned their basic addition and subtraction facts. Yet in the same class, Mr. Fenwick has another nine students who have been identified as being eligible for special services for the gifted and talented.

"I should be thankful," Mr. Fenwick tells himself. "Yes, it's a group with many academic deficiencies, but it's also a very *nice* group. There are no thieves, no pathological liars. Things could certainly be worse."

To accommodate the diverse academic needs of his class, Mr. Fenwick has his students working independently or in small groups much of the time so that they can all work on tasks tailored to their specific academic needs. A number of his students have difficulty staying on the tasks he's given, yet he is hardly in a position to keep his eye on everyone all of the time.

Although it's only October, Mr. Fenwick can already see behavior problems escalating in his classroom. He seeks the advice of the school psychologist, Ms. Rashad, who suggests that he consider using principles of behaviorism to encourage on-task behavior. Together the two of them identify a strategy that Mr. Fenwick might be able to use with the entire class.

The following morning, Mr. Fenwick brings to school a bag of marbles and a large, empty jar. Holding the jar and marbles up for everyone to see, he says, "Boys and girls, I've brought this jar and these marbles to help us get our work done." When the children look puzzled, he adds, "Every time I see someone in the room doing what he or she is supposed to be doing, I will put a marble in the jar. I will also put one in every time I see someone doing something to help someone else learn."

Gillian raises her hand. "You mean, every time we learn something, we get a marble?"

"That's right," Mr. Fenwick responds. "And when the jar is full, the whole class gets a reward—perhaps an ice cream party, a field trip, or an afternoon of fun and games in the classroom."

"Cool!" several of the children shout. A couple of them exchange high-fives.

"What reward shall we work for the first time?" Mr. Fenwick asks. He writes a number of possibilities on the chalkboard. Through a series of votes, the children narrow down the choices and eventually settle on a trip to the neighborhood firehouse as something that they would all enjoy.

---

[1]This case is derived from an unpublished case study written by Barbara Day.

In the days that follow, Mr. Fenwick keeps a lookout for appropriate and productive behaviors. Every time he drops a marble into the marble jar, he explains why he is doing so: "I see that all of you are hard at work on your reading assignments." "Thank you, Fernando, for helping James with his math problems." "You've all cleaned up your desks so nicely. Who would guess that just five minutes ago there were crayons, bottles of glue, and scraps of paper scattered everywhere?"

As the weeks roll on, Mr. Fenwick finds his children's classroom behavior slowly improving. Eventually, some behaviors occur so regularly that he decides that he probably doesn't need to reinforce them as frequently as he has in the past. At the same time, he adds new behaviors—for example, returning to one's seat promptly after recess, respecting other people's property, being a good listener—to his list of those that merit a marble when he sees them.

Possible questions for "The Marble Jar":

1. What basic principle of behaviorism is Mr. Fenwick using in this situation?
2. A reinforcement is an act of following a particular response with a reinforcer and thereby increasing the frequency of that response. Characterize the nature of the reinforcement that Mr. Fenwick is using.
3. Why do you think the marble jar is effective in improving students' behavior changes in Mr. Fenwick's classroom?

CASE 13
The Morning Routine

Every morning, Ms. Parker's second-grade class follows a predictable routine. Each of the reading groups meets with Ms. Parker for about 20 or 30 minutes. When children are not in their reading groups, they have several tasks to accomplish at their desks: They need to write the week's spelling words ten times each, complete three pages in their phonics workbooks, fill in a "following-the-directions" worksheet, and practice their addition facts.

This particular morning, Seeley is confused about her spelling words. She has already learned how to spell words such as *cap*, *tap*, and *mad*, but now the same words seem to have the letter *e* at the end of them (*cape*, *tape*, *made*). She vaguely remembers Ms. Parker saying something yesterday about how the words this week follow the "silent *e*" rule, but she can't recall what the rule is. Instead of informing her teacher about her confusion with the new rule, she reprimands herself, "Seeley, pay attention! You need to listen more carefully!" Then she just copies each word ten times and pulls out her phonics workbook.

For two weeks now, the phonics worksheets have been providing practice with consonant blends. Today's worksheets focus on *l* blends such as *pl*, *bl*, *cl*, and *fl* in words such as *plate*, *block*, *clock*, and *flower*. At the top of the first worksheet, Seeley sees a picture of a clock and the letters o c k with two blanks in front of them ("_ _ o c k"); she dutifully writes the letters *c* and *l* in the blanks. Next she sees a picture of a flower followed by "_ _ o w e r."

As Seeley finishes her phonics assignment, she hears her reading group being called to the reading table at the front of the room. Before the group starts reading, Ms. Parker reviews the "silent *e*" rule once again, but Seeley is still confused. "How can I read the words out loud when I must do it silently?" she thinks. When it is her turn to read, she mispronounces every word that ends in "silent *e*," often reading nonsensical sentences as a result. After Ms. Parker patiently corrects each mispronounced word, Seeley repeats the correct pronunciation and then continues with her reading.

Back at her desk, Seeley takes out her crayons and her following-the-directions worksheet. Today's sheet is similar to many others she's completed this year. It has a line drawing of a train engine, with the numerals 1, 2, 3, and 4 inserted at different spots. At the bottom of the page is a number-color scheme: 1 = red, 2 = yellow, 3 = blue, and 4 = black. Because the scheme is always the same, Seeley knows how to do the worksheets by heart. She colors all the "yellow" sections first, then the "blue" sections, then the "red" ones, and finally the "black" ones. She completes the task within five minutes.

Seeley polishes off her addition facts just as quickly. Now that she has finished her morning assignments, she knows that she has a choice between coloring quietly at her desk or going to the Listening Center at the back of the room to listen to a tape-recorded story. Today Seeley sits down at the Listening Center, puts a pair of earphones on her head, inserts a tape into the cassette player, and pushes the "play" button. Within five minutes, she is fast asleep.

Possible questions for "The Morning Routine":

1. Using ideas from cognitive views of learning, evaluate the effectiveness of Ms. Parker's morning routine.

2. How might Ms. Parker place each of the skills sets she wants her students to learn—spelling, phonics, following directions, and addition facts—within a more authentic context?

3. Seeley continues to be confused after two explanations of the "silent e" rule. What strategies might Ms. Parker use to make sure that her students **do** understand the rule?

4. Why do you think Seeley is falling asleep in class?

5. Like many children her age, Seeley blamed herself when she did not understand her teacher (i.e., concerning the "silent e" rule). How can you make sure your students are comprehending what you are saying?

CASE 14
Culture Shock

Mr. Beezley has been an elementary school teacher for many years, but teaching school in a small agricultural town in northwestern New Mexico is a new experience for him. Although he's been in town since early July, he hasn't attended any of the social events—the chili suppers, the donkey basketball game, the fall festival organized by the high school students—in the local community. By September, he's developed a reputation as a cold and arrogant Easterner.

Little does the community realize that Mr. Beezley is feeling quite overwhelmed in his new teaching position. Most of his students are Navajo children with very different backgrounds than those of his former students back in Massachusetts. He spends his evenings and weekends reading everything he can about Navajo culture, and he spends hours upon hours developing lessons and activities to meet the academic needs of his new students.

The classroom behaviors of Mr. Beezley's students present an additional challenge. Many of the children seem to have trouble staying in their seats and working independently. Mr. Beezley is quite surprised one day early in the school year when one of the boys in his class gets out of his seat to help another boy with a geography assignment. He approaches the two students to see if they need help, but they continue to talk to each other as if he weren't even there. He is shocked by their bold behavior. Back in Massachusetts, his presence alone would have been enough to silence any misbehaving students. At a loss for how to respond, he decides to do nothing for the time being.

A few minutes later, two other boys leave their seats to work with classmates. Having had enough of such behavior, Mr. Beezley reprimands them for getting up without permission. The boys are visibly shocked at his behavior, yet Mr. Beezley has never seen children so blatantly disrespectful. He angrily snatches the assignments on which the two students have been collaborating and insists that they return to their seats.

A few children are obviously quite upset by their teacher's actions, and so other children go to comfort them. Mr. Beezley can't believe that anyone has the nerve to get up after all that has happened. The continuing misbehaviors of his students utterly astonishes him.

"In my classroom, I expect you all to do your own work," he tells his class firmly. "Why are you all so insistent on doing everyone *else's* work?"

"We always help one another...," Maria responds.

"...Because it's the right thing to do," John continues, completing Maria's thought.

"How can we learn anything...," says Anna.

"If one of us doesn't understand?" adds Victor.

"Good grief," Mr. Beezley thinks to himself, "these children answer questions as a collective group. They can't even *talk* as individuals!" He is so taken aback by the fact that his students are rudely interrupting one another that he doesn't even hear what they are telling him.

Determined to nip the children's inappropriate behavior in the bud, Mr. Beezley goes to the main office after school to seek the advice of the school principal. Waiting patiently while the principal finishes a telephone conversation, he suddenly finds several of his students standing in front of him with their parents.

"Come...," says one of the parents.

"...and join us for dinner...," adds another parent.

"...for it will give us a chance...," continues a third.

"...to get to know one other," finishes a fourth.

Mr. Beezley is totally confused. Does everyone live in the same house? Or, on the other hand, is he supposed to go to four different homes for dinner in a single evening?

That evening, after following the parents' directions to the nearby Navajo Nation, Mr. Beezley finds himself at the home of one of his students. As he approaches the front door, he hears a great deal of laughter coming from the house. He expects to find a party inside but discovers that it is merely a gathering of several of his students' families sitting around a large table. The children's parents are telling tales from their own childhood, and one often interrupts another to insert additional anecdotes. They welcome Mr. Beezley to sit down, and for the next two hours he is enthralled by their colorful conversation. He discovers many aspects of Navajo culture about which he had been completely unaware—for example, how different families often live very intermingled lives.

After dinner, when a neighbor's truck breaks down, the entire group comes to the man's aid. Two parents go to town for the necessary parts, and on their return, the entire group works to repair the engine. Several people hold lights while others work under the hood and still others stand by to give advice.

By this time, Mr. Beezley feels comfortable enough that he is laughing and joking with the others. But he realizes that he still has a great deal to learn about the Navajo culture. He suspects that he'll learn as much from his new students as they are likely to learn from him in the days to come.

NOTE: Mr. Beezley spent many hours at the Navajo Nation after that, and he was always greeted affectionately when he arrived. He was frequently invited to join the Nation's sacred rituals, and he eventually became an honorary member of the community.

Possible questions for "Culture Shock":

1. *Should Mr. Beezley change his expectations for students' classroom behavior in his new teaching situation? Why or why not?*
2. *In general, to what extent is it appropriate for teachers to adjust their expectations and teaching practices to the cultural backgrounds of their students?*
3. *Might there be occasions in which Mr. Beezley should insist that his students work independently?*
4. *Mr. Beezley has difficulty making sense of the dinner invitation from his students' parents. Explain his difficulty using the notion of knowledge construction.*
5. *Beginning teachers are often so busy preparing their daily lessons and familiarizing themselves with school procedures that they lose sight of the larger community within which they work. As a new teacher, how might you get to know something about the culture or cultures in which your students have been raised?*

CASE 15
A Silent World

Fed up with the fast-paced lifestyle of southern California, Lynn Budzynski and her ten-year-old daughter Becky have just moved to Sugar Springs, a small town in the Rocky Mountains. Two days after their arrival, Ms. Budzynski brings her daughter to Sugar Springs Elementary School. She fills out the paperwork to enroll Becky, then asks Ms. Bohlender, the school secretary, if she can speak with the interpreter for hearing impaired students.

After pausing to think for a moment, Ms. Bohlender smiles and says, "Why don't you both have a seat for a minute? Let me see if I can find someone to speak with you."

Lynn turns to her daughter and repeats, both verbally and in sign language, what the secretary has just said, then mother and daughter sit down on a couch by the office doorway. Ms. Bohlender disappears down a hallway behind the counter and returns soon after with a man whom she introduces as Mr. Hardwick, the school principal.

Mr. Hardwick smiles at Lynn and Becky. "Welcome to Sugar Springs Elementary School. I'm afraid that we don't have an interpreter at our school right now, but I'll get on the phone this morning to make arrangements for one. In the meantime, why don't we get Becky started in her classroom so she can get acquainted with her new teacher and classmates? I think the best place to put her might be Mr. Matherson's fifth-grade class."

Mr. Matherson is caught completely off guard when Becky arrives at his door a short time later. As someone who has grown up in the same small town in which he now teaches, he has never before met someone who is deaf; as a result, he has no idea how to communicate with his new student. While Becky stands at the front of the room waiting for instructions on where to sit, she watches her new teacher push a button in a metal box on the wall and then speak to it.

While Mr. Matherson is busy with the box, Becky observes the other children in the room. Some of them are talking with one another, whereas others are staring at her. She jumps, startled, when her teacher comes up behind her and unexpectedly puts his hand on her shoulder. The other children seem amused by her reaction. Mr. Matherson looks at her and points towards the door.

"Oh, whew!" Becky thinks. "I'm in the wrong place." She starts to walk out the door, but her departure is blocked by a desk that the custodian is carrying inside the classroom. As she tries to walk around him, Mr. Matherson gently grabs her by the arm. The custodian sets the desk in the front row, winks at her, and walks out of the room. Mr. Matherson gestures for Becky to sit down at her new desk.

Before Becky arrived, the class had been in the middle of a lesson on long division, and the lesson now resumes. Seeing that the other children have their math books open on their desks, Becky signs for a textbook of her own. Mr. Matherson shrugs his shoulders to indicate that he doesn't know what she wants. Becky points to another child's book and then to herself. Mr. Matherson smiles and hands her a math book from a pile on the bookshelf.

Mr. Matherson says something to the class, then he writes a long division problem on the chalkboard. He slowly works through the problem, talking to the class as he does so. The other students occasionally nod their heads to indicate that they understand what he is showing them; observing their actions, Becky nods as well. Because she mastered the process of long division last year in California, she has no trouble understanding the process her teacher is demonstrating.

Mr. Matherson writes three more long division problems on the board. Becky sees several of the other children raising their hands, so she raises her hand as well. Mr. Matherson calls on two other children, who go up to the board and begin working on the first two problems. Mr. Matherson then points to Becky, motions for her to come forward, and directs her to the third problem. Understanding what she is supposed to do, Becky grabs a piece of chalk and solves the problem with ease. As she and the other two children return to their seats, the girl sitting behind Becky smiles at her and gives her a "thumbs up" sign.

Mr. Matherson talks to the class for a few minutes longer and then stops. Becky sees her classmates pull sheets of paper out of their desks and begin to write down several long division problems. She gives Mr. Matherson a puzzled look because she doesn't know where the problems are coming from. Finally realizing that his new student would not have heard the instructions he just presented, he writes on the chalkboard, "Do problems 8–20 on pages 58 and 59."

Becky pulls a sheet of notebook paper from her backpack and quickly completes the assigned problems. When she is finished, she looks around the room and sees that most of her classmates are still hard at work. After waiting patiently for a few minutes, she leans across the aisle to see how the boy next to her is doing. Mr. Matherson comes up to her, puts his hand on her shoulder, waves his index finger back and forth, shakes his head no, and then points to her paper.

Not understanding, Becky gazes at a bulletin board at the side of the room until Mr. Matherson walks away. Then she gently tugs at the shirt of the boy beside her in an attempt to get his attention. He doesn't seem to notice her, so she tugs his shirt a little harder. When he still doesn't look her way, she smacks him on the arm in desperation and points to an incorrect math problem. The boy yelps in pain and pushes Becky away from him. Mr. Matherson is instantly at Becky's side once again. She smiles at him as she watches him move his lips and shake his index finger at her. Although she's confused by her teacher's reaction, she's pleased that she's finally learned how to get people's attention.

Suddenly, the children head for the back door. Before Becky can get out of her seat to join them, she feels a familiar hand on her shoulder. Mr. Matherson motions for her to remain at her desk while the other children leave the room. Through the open door, she can see playground equipment and so correctly guesses that it's time for recess. Yet Mr. Matherson insists that she sit at her desk for several minutes before he permits her to join her classmates outside. She doesn't understand why she has to miss some of her recess.

As Becky surveys the school grounds, she sees most of the girls in her class standing in small groups and talking. Because she has no way of communicating with them, she decides not to join them. Instead, she walks over to the swings and stands beside a girl in a red jacket to wait for a turn. She gently touches the girl's sleeve, but the girl doesn't seem to notice her. Becky pinches the girl to get her attention; the girl turns around with a scowl on her face and then says something while holding her fist close to Becky's face. Becky is delighted to get the girl's attention and so smiles at her new "friend." When the girl turns to talk to someone else, Becky pinches her again. This time the girl runs to Mr. Matherson and points to Becky.

Over the next three days, Mr. Matherson continues to see instances of inappropriate behavior in Becky's actions. For example, she frequently looks at her classmates' work, a response that he interprets as cheating. In addition, her hitting and pinching other children to get their attention seems to have escalated. Mr. Matherson has used his usual bag of tricks to try to discourage the problem behaviors—he has tried tapping her on the shoulder, shaking his head, scolding her, keeping her in the classroom during recess—but nothing seems to be making a difference. He's at a loss as to what to do next.

During lunch time of Becky's fourth day at her new school, a young woman appears at the cafeteria door and speaks briefly to Mr. Matherson. She then approaches Becky, stoops down, and signs with her hands, "Hi, I'm Miss Hunter. I'm your new interpreter. Instead of going to recess after lunch today, how about if you stay inside with me so that we can get to know each other?"

Smiling, Becky signs, "Okay."

Becky is delighted that she finally has someone with whom she can communicate. She has many questions to ask, but she starts with the one that's puzzling her the most. "Why do I have to stay in from recess every day? Is it because my teacher doesn't like me?"

"I'm sure that Mr. Matherson likes you very much, Becky," Miss Hunter responds. "I don't know why he's keeping you in from recess. Perhaps we can ask him after he finishes his lunch."

When the rest of the class returns from their lunch break, Becky returns to her seat. As the afternoon's lessons proceed, Miss Hunter continually uses her hands to interpret what Mr. Matherson and the other students are saying.

At one point during a lesson on air pollution, Mr. Matherson asks, "What happens when fog and smoke in the air mix together?" Miss Hunter translates the question for Becky, and Becky quickly shoots her hand in the air. Mr. Matherson points in her direction. She signs to Miss Hunter, who translates for the class, "We get smog."

Mr. Matherson smiles at her and says something in response, which Miss Hunter signs as, "Good job, Becky. You're the only one who knew that."

Becky beams with pleasure and signs back to Miss Hunter, "*Anybody* from California would know that!"

After school, Mr. Matherson and Miss Hunter finally have a few minutes to touch base on how the two of them can help Becky change her inappropriate social behaviors. "She's trying to make new friends, but she hasn't had any luck," Miss Hunter explains. "For example, she told me that the other day she tried to help the boy next to her with his long division, but it only seemed to upset both him and you. I think that perhaps Becky just wants to interact with her classmates, but she doesn't know how to go about it."

"So maybe *that's* why she's been hitting and pinching the other kids so much," Mr. Matherson responds. "We...the children and I...thought that Becky was being too aggressive. We need to do something to help Becky and her classmates communicate more effectively."

"How about if I teach you and the other kids to sign?" Miss Hunter suggests.

The following morning, Miss Hunter begins the first of what will be many 30-minute lessons on American Sign Language. Among the first sentences that Miss Hunter teaches the class are, "Would you like to play with me?" and "Would you help me?" She also teaches them to coach Becky on more appropriate attention-getting behavior by saying such things as, "That's not nice. This is what friends do...."

At recess a short time later, Becky pinches a boy on the monkey bars. He immediately turns to her to sign, "That's not nice." He takes Becky's hand, places it on the monkey bars, then signs, "Better. Friends play together—not hurt each other."

Possible questions for "A Silent World":

1. *Operant conditioning occurs when a response increases after being followed by a reinforcing consequence. What instances do we see of operant conditioning in this case study?*

2. *Why are Mr. Matherson's attempts to punish Becky not having an effect on the behaviors he's trying to discourage?*

3. *What instances of modeling do we see in the case study?*

4. *On what occasion does Becky's behavior illustrate that she is accustomed to somewhat different standards for appropriate classroom behavior than exist in Mr. Matherson's class?*

5. *How might Mr. Matherson have better helped Becky adapt to her new classroom?*

CASE 16
Seven Chips[2]

E. Jefferson Ingersoll, III, was born with neurofibromatosis, a neurological disorder sometimes known as elephant man's disease. Jefferson's disease has affected his appearance; his head is a bit larger than usual, and many internal lesions have left discolored patches of skin on his arms and legs. The disease has affected his behavior as well: he walks a little off-center, and his movement is almost invariably awkward and unbalanced.

Unfortunately, Jefferson's doctors have been unable to determine the severity of his condition. They have warned his mother that neurofibromatosis often becomes progressively debilitating as the years go by and that Jefferson may not live to adulthood. Ms. Ingersoll has responded by trying to give her son a lifetime's worth of gifts and attention in the few short years that she may have him. The result is that when Jefferson begins third grade in Ms. Stanton's classroom, he is an overindulged boy who seems completely unable to regulate his own behavior.

From the first day of school, it is clear that Jefferson wants nothing more than to be liked by his teacher and classmates. At the same time, he seems to do everything possible to undermine his chances of gaining anyone else's affection. For example, he often interrupts the flow of small-group and whole-class lessons with inappropriate comments, irrelevant questions, or unprovoked laughter. During any single independent activity, he sharpens his pencil at least five or six times, always taking the most indirect route possible to the pencil sharpener; as he does so, he often bumps into someone else, necessitating either an excessively loud apology or a denial that he is in any way responsible for the mishap. And throughout the day, Jefferson makes frequent trips to the drinking fountain and the restroom, always managing to disrupt classroom activities in the process.

At first, Ms. Stanton tries to ignore Jefferson's inappropriate responses, thinking that such responses will gradually decrease if she refuses to reinforce them with her attention. But when she sees no improvement in his behavior, she tries other, more assertive strategies. For example, she praises him for on-task behavior while also reprimanding him for behaviors such as getting out of his seat, making inappropriate remarks, or in other ways disrupting classroom activities. On several occasions, Ms. Stanton meets with Jefferson and his mother to discuss the seriousness of the misbehaviors and to stress the importance of staying on task and allowing other students to do likewise. At one point, Ms. Stanton even develops a contingency contract for Jefferson, specifying desired behaviors in concrete terms and identifying the rewards that would follow such behaviors. Despite all her efforts, Jefferson's disruptive behaviors continue unabated.

---

[2]This case is derived from an unpublished case study written by Barbara Day.

While her class is at physical education class one afternoon, Ms. Stanton seeks the advice of Mr. Manzini, the school psychologist. Together they decide that, of all Jefferson's misbehaviors, his continual movement around the classroom is the most disruptive of all and so must be dealt with first. Mr. Manzini suggests that Ms. Stanton give Jefferson seven plastic poker chips at the beginning of school each day. Whenever Jefferson gets out of his seat without permission, he must "pay" for this behavior with a chip. Once he's used all seven chips, he must remain in his seat for the rest of the morning; a single out-of-seat behavior at this point will result in his having to spend the next lunch and recess alone in a small room just off the main office.

The following morning, Ms. Stanton describes the new procedure to Jefferson and gives him his first daily supply of chips. After that, whenever she sees him moving about the classroom without permission, she gets his attention and holds out her hand, and he obligingly gives her a chip. In the weeks that follow, Jefferson always limits his out-of-seat behaviors to the magic number seven. In fact, some days he doesn't even spend all the chips that he has. Ms. Stanton collects any extras at the end of each day, and then gives him a new pencil every time she's accumulated 25 of them.

Jefferson soon learns that if he gets out of his seat quietly and without disturbing his classmates, Ms. Stanton doesn't ask him for a chip. In fact, at one point, not only does she not request a chip, she also tells him, "I'm so pleased to see you moving quietly around the classroom, Jefferson."

Jefferson is immediately on the defensive. "It's okay for me to be out of my seat, Ms. Stanton. I still have a chip."

On one occasion, Jefferson is working at the back of the classroom with Ms. Zhang, the speech pathologist. When Ms. Zhang asks him to speak more softly, he asks her what she means.

"Talk like you do when you're doing independent work," Ms. Zhang responds. "You know...*whisper!*"

Jefferson laughs. "I only do that so Ms. Stanton won't take a chip," he exclaims loudly. Only when Ms. Zhang assures him that she, too, can take a chip does he lower the volume of his voice.

As the school year draws to a close, Jefferson still doesn't seem to be able to regulate his own classroom behavior. The seven daily chips work wonders in helping him keep his behavior under control. But when he receives no chips first thing in the morning—for example, when Ms. Stanton is suddenly called out of town and doesn't have a chance to brief the substitute teacher—he reverts back to his loud and disruptive actions. And when Jefferson enters Mr. Quinton's fourth-grade classroom the following year, it's as if he had never seen a poker chip in his life.

Possible questions for "Seven Chips":

1. *Characterize Ms. Fenwick's chip strategy using concepts and principles from behaviorism.*

2. *What evidence do we see that Ms. Fenwick's strategy, although leading to a temporary improvement in Jefferson's behavior, is unlikely to have long-term effects?*

3. *A **contingency contract** is a formal agreement between a teacher and student that specifies acceptable behaviors the student must demonstrate and the reinforcers that will follow those behaviors. When Ms. Fenwick develops a contingency contract for Jefferson, she violates one of the basic guidelines for such contracts. What mistake does Ms. Fenwick make?*

4. *What other strategies might a teacher use with a student like Jefferson?*

CASE 17
The Distracting Influence

Ms. Johnson has just convened the "Gorillas," one of the reading groups in her fourth-grade classroom. "Okay," she begins, "yesterday we started a new book, *The Phantom Tollbooth*, by Norton Juster. Who can summarize what happened to Milo in Chapter 1?"

As one of the Gorillas provides a summary for the group, Ms. Johnson overhears Nicole and Ashley talking and giggling at the front of the room. The girls should be silently reading Louis Sachar's *Wayside School Is Falling Down*. In fact, Ashley, who is visually impaired, has a Braille version of the book lying open in front of her.

Ms. Johnson doesn't mind her students occasionally talking with one another when the reading groups are meeting, as long as they do so quietly and are able to finish their assigned reading before recess. But Nicole has a habit of talking so much that she doesn't get her work done, and Ms. Johnson must often keep her in at recess to finish it.

Attempting to discourage Nicole's excessive chattiness, Ms. Johnson has moved the child's desk three times in the past two months. After the first move, Nicole sat next to Raul, a shy, quiet boy who always did his work. Unfortunately, Raul began modeling Nicole's behavior rather than vice versa, and within a couple of weeks the two children were talking and laughing most of their mornings away, to the point where Ms. Johnson was keeping them *both* in at recess to finish their classwork.

Ms. Johnson then moved Nicole to the other side of the room, seating her next to Peter. Although now a more sociable child than before, Raul was once again completing his assignments. In the meantime, Peter, rejected by most of his classmates as being too much of a bully, delighted in the friendship that Nicole offered him. In one respect, Nicole was a positive influence on him, showing him how to engage in friendly small talk with his peers. But like Raul, Peter usually became so engrossed in his daily conversations with Nicole that his classwork began to suffer.

Trying to harness Nicole's gift for gab, Ms. Johnson has finally moved the girl to the front of the room to sit by Ashley, hoping that Nicole could become a tutor of sorts, describing things that Ashley could not see. Today, for example, Nicole might describe the pictures in *Wayside School Is Falling Down*. But the girls' conversation today seems to be about rollerblading, rather than about the book. It's becoming increasingly clear that Nicole cannot keep her mind on her schoolwork no matter whom she sits with, and that, furthermore, she will always be pulling someone else off-task as well.

After wrapping up the Gorillas' discussion of new vocabulary words in *The Phantom Tollbooth*, Ms. Johnson distributes three-by-five index cards to each of her students. "Okay, class," she says, "before I convene the Tigers' group, I'd like for us to talk about a problem we seem to be having during reading group time. Some of you are off task too much when I'm meeting with one of the reading groups. What do I mean when I say *off task*?"

"Like talking to a friend," Aaron replies.

"Or sharpening our pencils all the time," Deion adds.

"Getting too many drinks at the fountain," Amanda says.

"Those are all good answers," Ms. Johnson observes. "*Off-task* behaviors are the things you do that keep you from getting your work done. Now on the card that I just gave each of you, I want you to write a checkmark every time you find yourself being off task while I'm working with the Tigers. Then do the same thing again while I'm working with the Pandas. This isn't a contest to see who has the most or the fewest checkmarks. It's just my way of helping you to help yourselves get your work done. It will also help you see exactly what you do with your time. Do you have any questions?"

"Will we get in trouble if our checkmarks show we're off task a lot?" Nicole asks.

"No, Nicole," Ms. Johnson replies. "Your cards are your own business; you don't even have to show them to me. It will be up to you if you want to share them with anyone or not."

Just before morning recess, Ms. Johnson asks, "Okay now, count up the number of checkmarks on your card. Let's go around the room and see how many checkmarks each one of you has. If you don't feel like sharing your number with the class, that's fine, too."

"Zero," says Janice.

"Two...well, three if you count goin' to the bathroom," says Bobby. The class laughs.

"Three."

"Two."

"Three."

"Zero."

"Zero."

"One."

Except for Nicole, all of the children announce how often they have been off task. The maximum number of checkmarks for any of them is three.

"You've been keeping track of your behavior for about an hour," Ms. Johnson says. "Do you think you were off task very much during that time?"

"No," most of the children shout. Ms. Johnson sees that Nicole is quiet and looking down at her desk.

Ignoring Nicole, Ms. Johnson smiles. "I agree, most of you were using your time wisely this morning. It's pretty neat to find out that you're doing your work without someone having to remind you all the time, isn't it?" After the children nod their heads in agreement, she continues, "Sometimes it's okay to be off task, like when you have to go to the bathroom. But sometimes it's *not* okay, like when you distract one of your friends by talking too much. Next time you find yourself off task, ask yourself, ' Is it worth it to do what I'm doing right now? Is it worth it to lose my recess time or to have to take my schoolwork home to do just because I want to goof off now'?"

While her classmates are playing outside, Nicole has, as usual, remained inside to finish up her reading. Ms. Johnson walks over to Nicole's desk and sits down beside her. "I wonder how you did with your checkmarks. Would you like to share your score with me?"

"Not really."

"You know, Nicole, the first step in changing a bad habit is awareness. If you aren't aware of what you're doing, you can't change your behavior. But my guess is that when you started keeping track of how often you were off task, you discovered that you were goofing off most of the time. Is goofing off really worth missing part of recess every day?"

"Ms. Johnson, until today...until we did the checkmark thing...I never realized *why* I was staying in from recess every day. I've always thought it took me longer to do my work because I'm not smart."

Ms. Johnson looks surprised. "Has someone ever *told* you that you weren't smart?"

"No. It's just that...well, ever since first grade, it seems as if I've always missed recess, or at least part of it, every day."

"Boy, that's an awful lot of recesses to be missing, isn't it? You know, I'll bet that once you start buckling down, you'll find that you're a pretty smart girl after all. What do *you* think?" Ms. Johnson pauses and looks Nicole straight in the eye. "Do you think you can try to keep yourself on task more often?"

"Yes!" Nicole replies. "I'm never going to talk in class again!"

"Well, that might be asking a lot of yourself, never to talk at *all*. But I would like you to continue keeping track of your own behavior during reading group time. How about if I let you borrow a digital timer I have that makes a little beep every five minutes? Each time you hear the beep, think about what you were just doing. If you weren't doing what you were supposed to be doing, then give yourself a checkmark."

"Okay. That seems easy enough."

"Well, I don't know if it will be easy, but I certainly know that you can do it."

In the days that follow, Nicole finds that she has fewer and fewer checkmarks each day. And after two weeks of monitoring her own behavior, Nicole enjoys her first full period of recess. By the third week, she no longer keeps tally cards. She is now able to stay on task regularly, and she hardly ever disturbs her classmates.

Possible questions for "The Distracting Influence":

1. *Prior to using the tally cards, what strategies does Ms. Johnson use to try to curb Nicole's off-task behavior?*

2.   *Explain the effectiveness of the checkmark strategy from the perspective of social cognitive theory.*
3.   *Self-efficacy is one's belief that one is capable of executing certain behaviors or reaching certain goals. Characterize Nicole's self-efficacy with regard to academic tasks.*
4.   *Is it appropriate for Ms. Johnson to ask her students to read their scores on the checkmark exercise aloud to the class?*
5.   *Is it appropriate to keep Nicole in from recess as a punishment for not completing her classwork?*
6.   *If you had a student like Nicole, what other strategies might you use?*

CASE 18
Throwing Tantrums

Although Tyler Lipton is listed on the roster of Allie Schenk's third-grade class, he spends most of each day in Sharon Osmer's resource room. Concerned that Tyler is so often segregated from his classmates, Allie has arranged a meeting with Sharon, Principal Cecila Dawson, and Tyler's parents.

Allie begins the meeting. "I'm concerned that Tyler is away from my classroom as much as he is. He's missing many of our instructional activities, and he has few opportunities to make friends with the other children in the class."

"Our son is severely dyslexic," explains Mr. Lipton, Tyler's father. "He's already repeated first grade, and now he's repeating second grade as well, yet he still can't read. I'd like him to spend as much time with Ms. Osmer as he possibly can."

"I worry about his behavior, too," Ms. Lipton adds. "Sometimes Tyler gets so frustrated that he throws horrible temper tantrums. It would never work to have him in a classroom with 25 other students. He needs as much individual attention as he can get."

Sharon Osmer is quick to agree. "Yes, Tyler's in my room so that we can address both his dyslexia and his behavior problems. I've had him for two years now, but his behavior is becoming even worse than it used to be. For example, he breaks pencils and tears his paper to shreds when he's frustrated or angry. Sometimes he screams when he doesn't want to do his work."

"Didn't Tyler's screaming start about the same time that you started working with Marcus?" Allie asks.

Sharon thinks for a minute. "Well, yes, now that you mention it, that's true."

"Who's Marcus?" inquires Ms. Lipton.

"Marcus is a boy with autism who's also in my room," Sharon replies. "He frequently screams and flaps his arms, especially when he's frustrated. It's pretty typical behavior for someone with autism."

"What do you do when Marcus screams?" Allie asks.

"Well," Sharon says, "as you know, I almost always have several students in my room at the same time, and each one of them is likely to have different academic needs. I usually give them individual assignments and put them at separate work stations around the room, then I circulate and give everyone a few minutes of one-on-one instruction. When Marcus gets too noisy, I pass out ear plugs so that the other students can concentrate on what they're doing. Then I try to find out why Marcus is so upset. He usually settles down after I've spent a little time with him."

"This meeting's about Tyler, not Marcus," Cecila Dawson reminds the group. "I think we should keep Marcus out of the discussion."

"Well, let me explain why I brought Marcus up," Allie says. "I talked with Kendra Westover, who had Tyler in her classroom two years ago, and she doesn't remember Tyler ever screaming in her classroom. She told me that he was placed in the resource room only for his reading problems, *not* for any behavior problems. So

I'm wondering...could it be that Tyler has learned to scream in your classroom, Sharon? After being with Marcus so much, he may think it's okay to scream when he's frustrated."

"Hmmm...that's an interesting idea," Ms. Lipton says. "Now that I think about it, I realize that Tyler's temper tantrums didn't really start until this year. Before that, he usually just talked to us when he was upset about something."

"I've been attributing his screaming more to his decreasing self-confidence," Mr. Lipton says. "Tyler's nine years old, and yet he still has trouble reading even the simplest words. He certainly doesn't feel good about that fact."

"I've been worried about his self-esteem as well," Sharon replies. "I've tried to boost it a bit by assigning him tasks that are easy for him. You know, completing color-by-number worksheets, listening to stories—things he can do successfully by himself. Yet his screaming seems to have increased rather than decreased."

"Sharon, you do wonderful things with the children you have in your resource room," Allie tells her. "But it sounds to me as if Marcus's behavior is rubbing off on Tyler. I'd like to suggest that we move Tyler back into my classroom for most of the school day. Perhaps you could give me some ideas about how I could help him with his reading skills."

"But you're forgetting about Tyler's behavior, Allie," Principal Dawson points out. "Tyler's a very disruptive child, and his presence in your room would be a great distraction. You must remember your other students. After all, they have the right to a classroom environment in which they can reasonably get some work done."

"It seems to me that Tyler needs to see how normal children behave," Allie observes. "I have a really good group this year—not a serious behavior problem in the bunch. How is Tyler ever going to learn appropriate classroom behavior when he's in a room with kids like Marcus all day?"

"I think you're being unrealistic, Allie," Principal Dawson says. "Tyler may feel ostracized when you put him with children who can read and write. By putting him in your classroom all day, we might destroy what little self-esteem he has."

"But there are many things that Tyler would be perfectly capable of doing in my classroom. For example, he could participate in science experiments. The children conduct the experiments in pairs, and he could certainly contribute. During reading times, he could listen to the other students read aloud and get involved in group discussions. And I see no reason why he shouldn't participate in physical education, art, and music along with his classmates."

Seeing that Allie is getting a bit hot under the collar, Principal Dawson tries to calm her down. "Now, Allie, I wasn't intending to ruffle any feathers. I'm just trying to point out that the approach you're suggesting might not be as easy as you think it will be."

Allie turns to Mr. and Ms. Lipton. "I have no idea what I can do for your son," she tells them bluntly. "I'm certainly no miracle worker. But it's clear that Tyler needs to learn to deal with his frustrations appropriately, and he can do that only if he interacts with regular kids on a regular basis. All I'm asking for is a chance to work with him. Will you at least think about it?"

Mr. and Ms. Lipton *do* think about it, and in a formal staff meeting later that month, the decision is made to place Tyler in Ms. Schenk's room for most of the school day. For a half hour each morning, when his classmates are meeting in their reading groups, Tyler will go to the resource room to work with Ms. Osmer on his reading skills.

Tyler has neither screamed nor torn up his work in the three weeks since he's joined Ms. Schenk's class. He still can't read or write at the same level that his classmates do—a continuing source of frustration for him. But he's making many new friends and cooperating well with others during group activities.

When Ms. Schenk asks Tyler why he used to scream in Ms. Osmer's class, his response is very revealing. "Well, wouldn't you get pretty upset if you had to do the same stupid worksheets and listen to the same dumb stories all day—*every* day—while all your friends get to do new and exciting stuff?"

NOTE: Tyler continued to be mainstreamed throughout his schooling. He is expected to graduate with his peers this spring (1997).

Possible questions for "Throwing Tantrums":

1.   *Using concepts from social cognitive theory, explain why Tyler begins screaming soon after he is placed in Sharon Osmer's classroom.*
2.   *What advantages are there in placing Tyler in Allie Schenk's classroom for most or all of the school day?*
3.   *Zone of Proximal Development (ZPD) is the range of tasks that a student can perform only with the assistance of a more capable individual. Using Vygotzky's concept of the ZPD, why are the tasks that Sharon Osmer assigns to Tyler developmentally inappropriate?*
4.   *How does Ms. Schenk predict that she can teach within Tyler's ZPD?*
5.   *If you were Tyler's teacher, what strategies might you use to accommodate his special needs?*
6.   *Self-esteem is the extent to which one believes oneself to be a capable and worthy individual. Sharon Osmer tries to enhance Tyler's self-esteem by giving him tasks that she knows he can accomplish successfully (e.g., color-by-number worksheets), yet Tyler's self-esteem continues to decrease. Why?*
7.   *Concerned that Tyler's academic needs are not being met, Allie schedules a meeting with the special education teacher, the school principal, and Tyler's parents. Is this an appropriate strategy? Why or why not?*

CASE 19
Keeping Track of Business

It's not unusual for students to have trouble adjusting to junior high school, so Ms. Cecere typically waits a couple of months after each new school year has started before contacting parents whose children are struggling in her classes. She makes an exception in Nathan's case, however, when she sees just how much difficulty he seems to be having from the very first day. Concerned about Nathan's progress, she arranges a meeting with Nathan and his parents, Mr. and Ms. Hamlin, one afternoon in early October.

Beginning the meeting, Ms. Cecere says, "I'm worried about how Nathan is doing in my German class. He has yet to turn in a test or quiz completed from start to finish; in fact, he usually leaves at least half of the items blank. It puzzles me, though. He almost always gets the questions that he *does* answer correct. And when I ask him about questions that he hasn't responded to, he seems to know the answers to them well enough."

"Sometimes I forget to finish my tests," Nathan explains. "I get distracted a lot."

"I'm like that, too," Mr. Hamlin observes. "I start thinking about other things and lose track of what I'm doing. Like father, like son, I suppose."

"I'm seeing a similar pattern in Nathan's other work," Ms. Cecere continues. "For example, he rarely completes the written exercises that I give in class each day. And when I look at my grade book, I see that Nathan hasn't turned in a single homework assignment all year."

"That surprises me," Ms. Hamlin says. "I make sure that Nathan works on his homework every night. In fact, last night, I helped him conjugate the three new verbs you assigned yesterday."

"Well, Nathan didn't turn that assignment in today," Ms. Cecere replies. Mr. and Ms. Hamlin look questioningly at their son.

"I thought that I handed it in," he tells them, "but I guess not."

"Nathan, I know you are a bright young man, because you always seem to have the right answer when I call on you. So I'm at a loss to explain why you're not getting your work done."

Mr. Hamlin pauses, seemingly gathering his thoughts together, and then speaks. "I think we should probably tell you, Ms. Cecere, that when Nathan was in second grade, he was diagnosed with a learning disability. He received special services in his elementary school's resource room for several years after that. But he seems to have licked a lot of the problems he had then. His mother and I would really like him to stay in your class."

Ms. Hamlin pats her son on the knee and adds, "I agree. I don't want him in any more resource rooms."

"Oh, I certainly don't want get rid of Nathan," Ms. Cecere assures them both. "On the contrary, I set up this meeting thinking that by putting our heads together, we might identify some strategies to help Nathan be more successful in my class. You said that Nathan received special services when he was in elementary school. What kinds of things seemed to work for him then?"

Ms. Hamlin opens her mouth to reply, but Nathan interrupts. "The doctor put me on drugs because the teachers said I was hyperactive. The drugs made me sleepy all the time. No more drugs!"

"We agree with you on that point," Ms. Hamlin responds. "There won't be any more drugs."

"What things did your resource room teacher do to help you with your schoolwork, Nathan?" Ms. Cecere asks.

"Well, let's see. Mostly she helped me with my reading. We worked on spelling a lot, and we worked on math some of the time. That's about it."

"I see. Did your teacher ever give you any suggestions to help you make sure you got your work done every day?"

"Not really, no."

Ms. Cecere thinks for a moment. "Well, I think that our best bet right now is to identify some ways to make sure that you *do* get your work done. For starters, let's have you use a small notebook to keep track of what assignments your teachers have given you and when each one is due."

Ms. Hamlin pulls such a notebook out of her purse. "Here's one I bought this morning for my grocery lists. Why don't you use it for your assignments, Nathan? I can always get another one for myself."

"It's perfect for what we need," Ms. Cecere observes. "Thank you, Ms. Hamlin. Now let's make three columns on the first page." Ms. Cecere draws two lines down the page and labels the three columns "Assignment," "Due Date," and "Done." I'd like you to write tonight's assignment—doing the exercise on page 58 of your textbook—in the first column under 'Assignment'."

After Nathan does so, Ms. Cecere continues. "Good. Now the next thing is to write the assignment's due date, which, in this case, is tomorrow, October 9th. Yes, just like that. You can use the notebook for your other classes, too, not just for German. Each night when you sit down to do your homework, use it to remind yourself about what you need to do. Every time you complete an assignment, double-check it to be sure that you have done *everything* that your teacher has asked you to do. Then put a checkmark beside the assignment in the "Done" column. Finally, when you turn in your work, but *only* when you turn in your work, you can pull out your notebook again and cross out the assignment altogether, because then you know that you don't have to worry about it anymore."

"I wonder if maybe either Alice or I should also check Nathan's homework to make sure that he hasn't left anything out," Mr. Hamlin offers.

"That's probably a good idea, especially until Nathan gets the hang of this new way of doing things."

"But what about when I'm doing assignments and stuff in class?" Nathan asks.

"I think you told me the other day that Forrest is in your German class, Nathan," Ms. Hamlin says to her son. "He's been your best friend since second grade. Maybe *he* wouldn't mind looking over your work. Would that be all right with you, Ms. Cecere?"

Ms. Cecere nods and then looks at Nathan. "What do you think of your mom's idea?"

"Yeah, sure. Forrest would probably do anything to keep me in the same class with him." The group laughs. "I might feel a little weird about it, though. Maybe, if I can do this notebook thing by myself, then I won't have to have him help me too much."

"Fair enough. Now what can we do about your quizzes and tests?" asks Ms. Cecere.

"I'll recheck each one to make sure that I've answered all the questions. That's something I've never done before. As a matter of fact, I think I'll check it at least twice before I turn it in to you."

"That's a good start, Nathan. And how would you feel if you and I met for a couple of minutes after every class in which you had a quiz or test? That way, I can look over your work with you before I grade it."

"Yeah, that'd be okay. But there's something else. If it's not asking too much, I'd really like to sit at the front of the room. It's hard for me to concentrate when I see everybody doin' other stuff in front of me. All I can think about is Freddie blowing his nose or Sheri passing notes. I guess I really need just to think about *German*."

"That's very perceptive of you, Nathan," Ms. Cecere commends him. "Forrest sits in the front row, so why don't you move up next to him. He's a good student, so I know he'll be able to keep you on task, if anyone can."

Three weeks after the meeting, Nathan's work habits have clearly improved. With the help of his notebook, his parents, his friend Forrest, and Ms. Cecere, he is regularly completing both his homework and his in-class assignments. But even the littlest classroom noises—a tapping pencil, a cough, the sound of someone using an eraser—still distract him during quizzes and tests. Ms. Cecere finds a quiet room down the hall where Nathan can take his quizzes and tests undisturbed, and his performance improves considerably. By the end of the semester, Nathan has earned a B in German, and he vows to Forrest that he can surely get an A in spring semester.

Possible questions for "Keeping Track of Business":

1. *What classic learning disabilities symptoms does Nathan exhibit?*
2. *In what ways does Ms. Cecere accommodate Nathan's special educational needs?*
3. *Based on her means of assessing her students' achievement, both formally and informally, how does Ms. Cecere define "good performance" in her class?*
4. *What other strategies might you use to assess students' achievement in a foreign language class?*

CASE 20
Summer School

To be honest, I accepted a summer school position at Cumberland Elementary because I thought the class would be an easy one to teach. I would have only five students and work half days, yet still get a full-time salary. But, as I soon discovered, I was sadly mistaken in my belief that the position would be an effortless one. For one thing, teaching five students with special needs was far more difficult than teaching a classroom of 30 so-called normal students. In addition, I discovered that there is probably no such thing as working only half a day when you're a teacher: After teaching my class every morning, I spent the afternoon creating individualized lessons to meet each child's specific academic needs in reading, writing, and mathematics. By the end of the first week, it was clear that my "part-time" job would consume my entire summer.

I don't think that I could have had five more different students if I had tried. Ben, who was nine, suffered from a progressive neurological condition that had left him blind and was slowly eroding his mental capabilities. Although usually a kind and gentle child, he would have unpredictable outbursts that disrupted whatever the rest of us might be doing. For example, several times a day, he would suddenly scream and start punching the air with his fists until he eventually found something solid—a desk, a wall, or perhaps another student. He would then continue punching that object or person until I physically restrained him. I didn't feel that I could reprimand Ben for such outbursts, as they were undoubtedly a symptom of his neurological impairment.

Eleven-year-old Hannah had been sexually molested by her mother's boyfriend on numerous occasions over the past two years, and she now displayed a variety of bizarre behaviors. For example, she would frequently reach out to touch or grab other students in inappropriate places. On several occasions, always when I was preoccupied with Ben, she would take off her clothes and rub her body against different objects around the room—her desk, her artbox, pencils, you name it. When she was nervous about something, she would compulsively rock back and forth in her chair, or she would pull at her hair until she left a bald spot.

Meanwhile, nine-year-old Cameron had a distinctly sadistic streak. He would hit his classmates, often on the nose or in the eyes, then smile as they screamed out in pain. He spit on people just to see how they'd react. If they expressed disgust, he'd spit on them again; if they lashed out in anger, he'd hit them and run away.

My other two students had been diagnosed as having mental retardation. One of them, Arnold, was a sweet-tempered eight-year-old who had Down's syndrome. The other, twelve-year-old Steven, had no genetic disorders but had been officially labeled as "mentally retarded" based on his low scores on a series of intelligence tests. Steven's prior schooling had been limited to just part of one year in a first-grade classroom in inner-city Chicago. His mother had pulled him out after a bullet grazed his leg while he was walking to school one morning; fearing for her son's safety, she would not let him outside the apartment after that, not even to play, and certainly not to walk the six blocks to school. When a truant officer finally appeared at the door one evening in May five years later, Steven and his mother quickly packed their bags and moved to a small town in northern Colorado. They found residence with Steven's aunt, who persuaded Steven to go back to school. After considering Steven's intelligence and achievement test scores, the school psychologist recommended that he attend my summer school class.

Perhaps my biggest challenge that summer was to keep my five students from physically harming one another. Numerous disputes occurred every day, often when I least expected them. For example, we might be in the middle of a lesson when, all of a sudden, one child or another would starting yelling and screaming in a classic temper tantrum.

One day especially stands out in my mind. We had been studying nutrition, and so I had asked each of the children to bring in some fresh vegetables to make a large salad for our morning snack. Steven arrived with a can of green beans.

"What the hell is that?" Cameron yelled from across the room. Cameron cursed frequently. Initially I had thought that he did it to gain attention, but I soon learned that cursing was the standard manner of speaking in his family. I usually ignored Cameron's foul language, reasoning that I had more important behaviors of his to change.

"It's green beans!" Steven stated proudly.

"What's goin' on?" asked Ben, who could not see what Steven had brought.

Hannah answered his question. "Steven brought a *can* of green beans."

"If they're in a can, then they're not fresh," Ben pointed out.

"The hell they ain't!" was Steven's angry reply. "Me and Momma got them off the shelf this morning!"

Oh my, I thought, what to do now? And then it suddenly hit me—Steven quite possibly wasn't mentally retarded at all! It was his prior knowledge—or rather, his *lack* of it—that was interfering with his academic progress. After all, he didn't even know what a "fresh" vegetable was. My mind was reeling, and mentally I was quickly revising my objectives for Steven. He needed to learn the basics—not only in reading, writing, and mathematics but also with regard to the many facts and concepts that most children his age had already acquired.

While I was pondering Steven's situation, Cameron darted across the classroom and whacked Steven's nose. "Stupid kid!" he yelled. "You don't even know what's fresh!"

Despite my best efforts to restrain Cameron, he continued to attack Steven all morning long. When Steven's mother arrived at noon to pick up her son, I shared the day's unfortunate events with her. Remembering why she had removed her son from first grade in Chicago, I fully expected her to remove him from my classroom as well. Instead, she told me, "Ms. Teacher, I think it's time we did something about this aggression. Recess ain't cuttin' it for these kids. They're all still too full of piss and vinegar to study."

"No kidding," I silently agreed while tightly holding Cameron's hands to keep him from inflicting further damage on Steven's body. The bus driver was standing in the doorway wondering why the four children he usually took home—Cameron, Hannah, Ben, and Arnold—weren't ready to leave. The bus driver's assistant picked up Cameron and carried him onto the bus. Hannah left the room flapping her arms. Ben was holding Arnold's left elbow and walking toward the bus when he suddenly grabbed Arnold's hair and gave it a quick yank.

"No pulling hair, Ben!" yelled Arnold. Ben momentarily fingered the strands of hair that he had pulled from Arnold's scalp. The strands drifted to the ground unnoticed, and Arnold continued to guide Ben towards the bus as though nothing had happened.

Maybe Steven's mother was right—maybe my students needed an outlet for all their pent-up energy, because recess simply wasn't "cuttin' it." I wondered if some vigorous physical activity first thing in the morning might relieve some of their energy. We tried everything, it seemed—kickball, basketball, tag, running races—yet I saw little improvement in their behavior when we finally settled down for academic work later in the morning. Then one day, I found plastic hockey sticks and a hollow plastic puck in the back of the gymnasium closet. I wasn't sure that I could trust my students with such potentially dangerous equipment, yet I decided to take a chance and teach them the basics of field hockey, albeit an in-door version of the game.

I knew that I needed to adapt the game for Ben, who was blind. So I had players on the "blue team" wear high-pitched Christmas sleigh bells tied around their wrists; players on the "red team" wore similar bells tied to their shoe laces. I sliced open the handles of the hockey sticks and inserted lower-pitched bells, then glued the handles shut again, so that Ben would be able to tell where each player's hockey stick was on the playing field. I put a loud buzzer inside the plastic puck. I attached electronic beepers to the tops and sides of the goals.

We went to the gym first thing each morning for a half hour of hockey. All five students really got into the game, and not one of them ever tried to hit a classmate with a hockey stick. Except for Ben, whose neurological condition seemed to worsen as the summer wore on, the aggressive behavior in my classroom completely stopped once we began our daily hockey games. I honestly don't know why. Maybe hockey provided more of an outlet for their energy than our other activities had. Maybe the game forced them to depend on one another in a way that they had never had to before. Maybe my allowing them to play with potentially dangerous equipment communicated a sense of trust that they didn't want to abuse. Maybe their change in behavior was just a fluke and had nothing to do with the hockey games at all.

Oddly, it was Cameron who taught me how to predict Ben's temper tantrums. One day, he said to me, "Teacher, I don't think Ben should be playin' hockey right now."

"Why not, Cameron?"

"He's getting ready to be mean."

"How do you know that?"

"Look at his ears. They get red whenever he's ready to hurt someone." I looked at Ben's ears and discovered that Cameron had described them accurately. I guided Ben over to the punching bag, where he proceeded to have a violent temper tantrum, taking much of his anger out on the bag. The other four children continued their hockey game as if nothing out of the ordinary were happening.

With their energy expended in the gym first every morning, we actually had time to focus on more academic tasks. Steven improved by leaps and bounds that summer; he was like a sponge that absorbed as much as he possibly could. The others made a little progress on their reading, writing, and mathematics, although probably not enough to brag about. On the other hand, all five of my students made dramatic gains in their social skills. By the end of the summer, each of them was able to express anger in an appropriate verbal fashion instead of striking out physically.

NOTE: By the time Steven reached high school, he was enrolled in regular classes and maintained a 3.5 average; the last time I spoke with his mother, she told me that he was planning to attend Indiana University the following September. Meanwhile, Hannah and Arnold remained in self-contained classrooms for several years to follow. Ben died a year after he left my classroom from complications due to his neurological condition. I have no idea what happened to Cameron.

Possible questions for "Summer School":

1. *When Cameron curses ("What the hell is that?"), his teacher ignores him. Is this an appropriate reaction to Cameron's inappropriate behavior?*
2. *At one point, the teacher concludes that Steven isn't mentally retarded at all. Is her conclusion an accurate one?*
3. *What benefits might the daily hockey games have had?*

CASE 21
Topography

Less than a week before the school year begins, Ms. Steinbach receives a telephone call from Ms. Rocco, the principal at Oceanside Middle School. "I'd like to offer you a job teaching social studies," Ms. Rocco tells her. "Are you interested?"

"Why, yes, I am," Ms. Steinbach answers, trying to keep her excitement from being too obvious in her voice.

"That's wonderful news," Ms. Rocco responds. "I was very impressed when I interviewed you last spring, but at the time I didn't think we'd be needing another social studies teacher. As it turns out, Mr. Richardson, whom I believe you met during your interview, has just resigned to take a job in another district."

The two women meet the same afternoon so that Ms. Steinbach can sign her contract and learn about the responsibilities of her new position. Ms. Rocco tells Ms. Steinbach that, among other things, she will be teaching two sessions of geography every morning. "Mr. Richardson ordered new geography textbooks for this year. I believe that there are two boxes of them stacked beside the door in your classroom."

Ms. Steinbach thanks her new principal and hurries to her classroom, well aware that she has many hours of planning and preparation ahead of her over the next few days. The two boxes of geography texts are exactly where Ms. Rocco had said they would be. Opening one of the boxes, she finds a teacher's manual resting on top of about 20 textbooks.

Sitting at her new desk, Ms. Steinbach grabs a copy of the textbook. As she flips through the pages, she is chagrined at what she sees. Each chapter seems to be mostly a collection of facts listed one after another in rapid succession. New concepts—*plateau, tundra,* the *Continental Divide*—are briefly defined but rarely explained in any detail. Little attempt is made to pull all the facts and concepts together into a coherent whole.

When Ms. Steinbach opens the teacher's manual, she is even more discouraged. The classroom activities it describes focus on basic skills—identifying cardinal directions (north, southeast, etc.), interpreting simple bar graphs, using scales to estimate distance—that she suspects her students have probably already mastered. The homework assignments that the manual provides are fill-in-the-blank exercises based on word-for-word excerpts from the textbook. And the quizzes for each chapter include only true-false and multiple choice items.

Having taken several geography courses in her undergraduate program, Ms. Steinbach knows perfectly well that geography is much more than facts and figures. She wants her students to learn broad geographic principles—principles that they can use to make better sense of the world around them. The textbook and teacher's manual aren't going to help her meet her objective, so she had better get busy developing alternative lessons and activities.

Throughout the fall, Ms. Steinbach tries a number of different strategies to make geographic principles come alive for her students. For example, when teaching students about topography, she brings in several raised relief maps and gives the class a "scavenger hunt" list of landforms (mountain ranges, plateaus, river valleys, foothills, and so on) to locate on the maps. When teaching her class about volcanic activity, she borrows a series of slides from the local university's geography department to depict what Mount St. Helens looked like before and after its eruption in 1980. During hurricane season, Ms. Steinbach uses the Internet to locate the National Weather Service's daily updates regarding the location and status of current tropical storms and hurricanes and then has her students plot the course of each weather system on a large map of the Atlantic Ocean and eastern seaboard states.

On another occasion, after puzzling for several days about how she can make the effects of elevation on rainfall more concrete than the textbook's explanation, Ms. Steinbach conducts a rather unusual activity. "Okay, class," she begins, "I need five volunteers to help us learn why the western side of a mountain usually gets more rainfall than the eastern side."

Many hands go up. Ms. Steinbach selects several of the more reserved students in her class—Angela, Miguel, Raymond, Tara, and Dee.

As the five volunteers walk to the front of the room, Ms. Steinbach places a bowl full of water on the floor. "Okay, Angela, this bowl is the Pacific Ocean. Now your name is perfect for what you need to do, because I want you to be Los Angeles. Lie down just to the right of the bowl, please, because Los Angeles is a city that lies just to the east of the Pacific Ocean." The class snickers a bit as Angela obligingly lies on the floor beside the bowl.

"Now, Miguel," Ms. Steinbach continues, "I'd like you to be the San Gabriel Mountains that rise up just to the northeast of Los Angeles." She gently moves Miguel so that he is standing to the right of Angela. "There, that's good. Just be careful that you don't step on Los Angeles." Again the class giggles.

Next, Ms. Steinbach looks at her third volunteer. "Okay, Raymond, I'd like you to be Barstow, a town that lies in the flatlands to the east of the San Gabriel Mountains." Catching on immediately to the nature of her request, Raymond lies down to the right of where Miguel is standing.

"Perfect!" Ms. Steinbach exclaims. "Okay, class, here we have southern California. You see before you the Pacific Ocean—the bowl of water—then Los Angeles, the San Gabriel Mountains, and the town of Barstow on the other side." She looks quickly at her students and notes that their eyes are all focused on the front of the room in eager anticipation of what will happen next in this rather unusual scenario.

"So now we need a cloud and some wind. Tara, let's make you the wind. Stand over to the left of the bowl there, somewhere out in the middle of the ocean. And Dee, I'd like you to be a cloud." Ms. Steinbach hands Dee a sponge and nudges her to a spot directly in front of the bowl. "As a cloud, you hold quite a bit of the water vapor that's evaporated from the Pacific Ocean. So take your sponge and suck up some of the ocean from the bowl there." Dee stoops down, places the sponge in the bowl, and then stands up with the sponge dripping with water.

"Excellent. So then, here we have an air mass full of water—a cloud—just hanging out over the Pacific Ocean. And then along comes the prevailing wind, the wind from the west, to move the cloud eastward. Okay, wind, blow away!" Tara dutifully blows on Dee's shoulder, and Dee walks slowly to the "east," holding the sponge over "Los Angeles" as she does so. Angela grimaces as a few drops of water land on her face, but says nothing. Just before Dee reaches the "San Gabriel Mountains" that are Miguel, Ms. Steinbach stops her.

"Now here's where things get interesting, folks. Notice that the cloud has to rise as it travels over the mountains. As it does so, it's going to get *cooler* and *smaller*, and it won't be able to hold as much water. So what happens now?"

"It'll start to rain!" Luke shouts out.

"Good, Luke. So, Tara, let's get the wind going again. And Dee, let's make that cloud smaller and smaller as it starts to go over the San Gabriel mountains." Tara resumes her blowing, and Dee slowly moves to the right once again, squeezing the sponge harder and harder as she does so. Angela and Miguel are being "rained" on in the process, but they are clearly enjoying the attention they are getting from their classmates as a result of their predicament.

"Now, then, the cloud starts going back down on the east side of the San Gabriel mountains and gets warmer again. What happens to the rain?"

"It stops!" Kathleen calls out.

"Right!" Picking up on her cue, Dee stops squeezing the sponge as Tara "blows her" to where Raymond is lying. "So look at poor Barstow. It's dry as a bone. Has anyone here ever been to Barstow, California?"

"I have," Kenneth responds. "My dad and I go there sometimes for the all-terrain vehicle races."

"So what's it like in Barstow, Kenneth?"

"Well, there's lots of sand and gravel, and hardly any trees. Like you just said, Ms. Steinbach, it's dry as a bone."

"Exactly." Ms. Steinbach looks pointedly at Raymond, who is still lying on the floor to the right of Miguel. "Mr. 'Barstow' here is smack-dab in the middle of the Mojave Desert."

Possible questions for "Topography":

1. *Why is Ms. Steinbach so discouraged when she looks at the textbooks and teacher's manual that Mr. Richardson ordered?*
2. *What strategies does Ms. Steinbach use to help her students learn effectively?*
3. *What strategies does Ms. Steinbach use to motivate her students and keep their attention?*
4. *Ms. Steinbach intentionally chooses some of the more reserved students to participate in the rainfall demonstration. What might be her rationale for doing so?*

5.   *Ms. Steinbach uses some rather creative strategies for making geography "come alive" for her students. What resources might you use to identify and develop equally creative strategies for teaching your own students?*

CASE 22
Climate

Ms. Marotta is a teacher education major who, in preparation for her student teaching next year, is now spending two hours every morning observing and assisting in a middle school geography class. At the request of her supervising teacher, Mr. Koehn, she's prepared a lesson about climate using the same interactive, question-answer format that she has watched Mr. Koehn use so effectively over the last few weeks. Ms. Marotta has just led the students through their geography textbook's chapter on climate and is now beginning to engage them in a follow-up discussion.

"How many of you have air conditioning?" she asks. About half of the students raise their hands.

"If you lived in Houston, how many of you would have air conditioning?" All but two of the students raise their hands.

Ms. Marotta glances briefly at her lesson plan. "Who can tell me what topic we talked about last Friday?"

"Temperature," says Germaine.

"Wind," says Marsha.

"Climate," says Tomas.

"Okay. On Friday, Mr. Koehn described several different things that affect climate. Who can tell me what they are?" When the students remain silent, Ms. Marotta continues. "What's the difference between where we are and Long's Peak (a 14,255 foot mountain in Colorado)?"

"Long's Peak is higher," Marsha says.

"Oh, yeah—*elevation*!" shouts Caitlin.

"Right, Caitlin. Elevation is one thing that affects climate. What's another one?"

"Latitude," Maya responds.

"Right. What effect does living near the water have?"

Janina whispers briefly to the girl sitting beside her and then raises her hand. "Cooler in summer, warmer in winter."

"Good, Janina. Water makes things cooler in the summer and warmer in the winter. All right, class, now open your books to page 48. Kevin, can you read the section called 'Polar Region' for us?"

Kevin is slow to find the section to which Ms. Marotta is referring. As he reads, he mumbles so much that hardly anyone can hear him. Too late, Ms. Marotta remembers that Kevin is one of the poorest readers in the class. "That's okay," she thinks. "The others can read the passage to themselves anyway."

"Who has good handwriting?" Ms. Marotta asks. "Okay, Jackson, you can be our recorder today." Jackson approaches the chalkboard smiling, obviously relishing the fact that he will be the center of attention for the next few minutes. He picks up a piece of chalk, poised to begin his recording duties.

"What are some things we've just learned about the polar region?" Ms. Marotta asks. "Jackson will write your answers on the board."

"Less sunlight," says Meghan.

"Especially in winter," Julian adds.

"The ground stays frozen," says Alan.

"Long, cold winters," says Will.

"Short summer," says B.J.

"*Cool* summer," says Reynelda.

"Did you get everything on the list?" Ms. Marotta asks Jackson. "Good, I see that you did. Okay, is there anything else we need to add?"

The children search their textbooks for other possibilities. "Not much precipitation!" shout Germaine and Arnie simultaneously.

"Why isn't there much precipitation?" Ms. Marotta asks.

"Because the air's so cold that it can't hold much moisture," responds Libby.

"So if you lived in Alaska, you'd have some days with very little sunlight and very long nights. What do you think it would be like to live in Alaska in the winter? How do you think you might feel?"

"Tired," says Alan.

"Lazy," says Meghan.

Ms. Marotta waits for a few seconds, but the students seem to have run out of ideas. "You might get very depressed, too, mightn't you?" Several students nod. "Okay, then, who would like to read the section about the 'Temperate Region' for us?"

The lesson continues as the class reads about temperate, subtropical, and tropical regions. As the students list the characteristics of each climactic region aloud, Jackson writes them on the board.

Glancing at her watch, Ms. Marotta realizes that the class period is almost over. "Thank you for taking notes for us, Jackson," she says. "Now did you all get the characteristics of the different regions in your notebooks?"

The students look at her with blank expressions. As she surveys the room, she realizes that none of the students has even opened a notebook. Early in the school year, Mr. Koehn had the class create sections in their looseleafs called "Geography." Why has it not occurred to anyone to take notes today? After all, Jackson has made the job easy for them by listing everything on the board.

As Ms. Marotta thinks about it, she recalls how Mr. Koehn has always told the class when to take notes and exactly what to write each time. "I guess I still have a lot to learn about teaching middle school students," she thinks to herself.

Possible questions for "Climate":

1.   *What strengths do you see in Ms. Marotta's lesson?*
2.   *What weaknesses do you see in Ms. Marotta's lesson?*

3. *Ms. Marotta inadvertently asks Kevin, a poor reader, to read a section of the chapter aloud. Is it a good idea to ask your students to read aloud? Why or why not?*

4. *Why do the students not take notes, even though Jackson has made it easy for them to do so?*

5. *Good teachers reflect about how their lesson has gone. How did Ms. Marotta reflect about her lesson?*

CASE 23
Solving Problems

Ms. Fieseler doesn't want her eighth-grade pre-algebra students just to memorize the mathematical procedures that she teaches them; she also wants them to be able to use those procedures to solve actual problems. So she frequently assigns word problems related to whatever topics are currently under discussion. In Ms. Fieseler's mind, the problems she assigns are pretty straightforward and sometimes downright obvious. Yet many of her students have difficulty solving them on their own. Thinking that they might be more successful if they work together, she decides to incorporate the problems into a cooperative group activity at the end of each week.

Today, Ms. Fieseler has instructed the cooperative groups to solve the following three problems:

Your parents have given you permission to redecorate your bedroom. You want to build a shelf for your books on the wall beside your bed. The wall is 15 feet across. Your dad has given you a lot of metal shelf brackets and some pieces of wood that are each 18 inches long, 6 inches wide, and 1 inch thick. How many pieces of wood will you need if you want to make one long shelf that goes across the entire wall?

Now you want to paint your bedroom. The paint comes in one-quart cans, and paint from a single can will cover about 200 square feet. If your bedroom is 15 feet long and 10 feet wide, and if your ceiling is 8 feet from the floor, how many cans of paint will you need?

You also want to lay new carpet in your bedroom. It costs $9.00 a square yard. How much will you need to buy carpet that covers the entire floor?

"Now remember, class," Ms. Fieseler tells her students, "your performance on your group problem-solving exercises will be worth one-third of your grade this fall. You need to work together to make sure everyone in your group understands what he or she is doing."

One group sitting in the far corner of the room includes four students—Jack, Leo, Elizabeth, and Olivia—who are highly motivated to do well on the assignment. The fifth group member, Seth, would rather be playing video games on the portable Nintendo he has hidden in his backpack than working on math problems with this bunch of "nerds."

"You're late, Seth," Elizabeth admonishes him as he approaches the table. "And get those pencils out of your nose. That is *soooo* gross!"

Leo and Olivia laugh at the walrus-like image that Seth has created. Seth grins, then transplants the pencils to his ears. Olivia rolls her eyes; the other three group members ignore his childish behavior.

"We're on the second part already, Seth," Leo says. "This one's about painting, and it's really hard. Your dad's a painter, isn't he? Come on, tell us what we should do."

Seth glances at the problem that Olivia is pointing to, then impulsively writes "101" in the margin beside it.

"Seth! What are you doing?!" Jack asks indignantly. "You just made the answer up, didn't you?"

"He has to be faking it," Elizabeth points out. "There's no way the answer can be so high."

"One hundred and one Dalmatians," Seth explains. "Get it?"

"What do Dalmatians have to do with this problem?" Leo asks. "Grow up, Seth!"

"Geez, you guys got no sense of humor," Seth responds. "Who cares about this stuff, anyway?"

"Seth, don't you care about your grades?" Elizabeth asks. "Even if *you* don't care, your parents probably do."

"Yeah, right! My folks don't give a s--- how I do in school. They'd think I was great even if I was robbin' banks."

"You guys, we need to get back to work," Leo reminds the group.

Seth scrawls "29" next to the third problem. Ignoring him, the other four students discuss the second problem at length and eventually reach the correct answer of "2 cans." They then struggle with the third problem but eventually conclude that they don't have all the information they need to solve the problem. At the end of the group session, the group turns in a sheet of paper that lists all five group members at the top and solutions to the first two problems.

"Ms. Fieseler, I'm gettin' tired of the same people doin' all the work when we're in groups," Jack complains.

"Yeah, it isn't fair," Elizabeth adds. "Only a few of us do the work, yet everyone gets credit."

"So what do you think we should do about the situation?" Ms. Fieseler asks.

The students expect their teacher to answer her own question, but she remains silent. Finally, Olivia proposes a solution. "I say we kick any goof-offs out of the group."

"Hmmm," Ms. Fieseler responds pensively. "Is that what people in the business world do?"

"Absolutely!" says Leo. "They fire anyone who's too lazy to help out. I think we should do the same thing—you know, 'fire' lazy people from our groups. They can do their *own* work."

"Sometimes people are stuck with one another," Linda points out from across the room. "Like, my mom has to work with this jerk who doesn't do anything except sit around and look smart all day. She's always complaining at home about how she has to pick up the slack."

"Linda's right," Ms. Fieseler tells the class. "You're basically stuck with one another in your cooperative groups. So how can we make sure that everyone participates constructively during group time?"

"I say we don't speak to anyone who *doesn't* help out," Mary Lou suggests.

"Maybe when we turn in the problem answer sheets we fill out, we should only let the people who have worked enough on the problems sign their names," Elizabeth says.

"Hmmm...how will we know what 'enough work' is?" Ms. Fieseler asks.

"If someone tries to help at least once, then that person is contributing to the group," Mary Lou answers.

"But how would you decide that the person has actually *contributed*?" Ms. Fieseler asks.

"Well, you know, if they seem like they're trying real hard, even if they're wrong, they're contributing," Joe volunteers. "And especially if they try to explain the steps they went through to solve the problem, then they're contributing."

"But what if somebody absolutely refuses to help out?" Leo calls out.

"Then they don't get the group reward," states Ms. Fieseler. "Remember, the group with the most points at the end of the month doesn't have to do any homework for a week."

Possible questions for "Solving Problems":

1. *Many mathematics teachers use word problems to help students transfer mathematical concepts and procedures to real-world contexts. Do you think word problems are an effective way of doing that? Why or why not?*

2. *Why does Seth's group conclude that it does not have all the information it needs to solve the third problem?*

3. *What are the potential benefits of assigning cooperative group activities as a way of helping the students learn how to solve mathematical problems?*

4. *There will always be students who, like Seth, hope to get a "free ride" during cooperative group time. What strategies might a teacher use to minimize such free rides?*

5. *Why do you think Seth is being uncooperative?*

6. *Does Ms. Fieseler resolve the "free rider" situation?*

7. *At the end of the case study, Ms. Fieseler tells her students, "The group with the most points at the end of the month doesn't have to do any homework for a week." Is this a good idea? Why or why not?*

CASE 24
Consequences

"Okay, class, it's time to turn in your spelling crossword puzzles," Ms. Wyatt announces to her sixth-grade class.

"But I didn't finish mine," Nicholas complains.

"Neither did I," adds Derek.

"Of course not!" Eldrick shouts out. "You guys were too busy talking about Cindy Crawford!"

"Well, you have to admit, she *is* something to talk about," Nicholas retorts.

Ms. Wyatt shakes her head in mock disgust. "Apparently puberty is settling in here, isn't it, class? Especially for a couple of boys I know." The class giggles, then she says, "Nick and Derek, I'd like you to finish your work when you have some free time after lunch." The two boys nod their heads to indicate that they will.

Assigned to groups of three, Ms. Wyatt's students have been working on their papier-mâché relief maps of North America for most of the afternoon. But one group—Molly, Helen, and Lori—has been so busy talking about their favorite television show that they have put little effort into completing their map.

"Hey, you guys," Molly urges, "we'd better get busy. We only have 20 more minutes left before we have to go to music."

"Ah, don't worry about it," Helen tells her.

"Yeah, we can always finish tomorrow," Lori adds.

Ms. Wyatt flicks the lights to get her students' attention. "Class, I forgot to tell you about the bonus today. The first group to finish its relief map will have 15 minutes of free time this afternoon."

"All *right*!" several of the children shout.

"Why didn't she tell us earlier?" Helen whispers to her friends.

"It drives me crazy when she does stuff like that," Lori whispers back. "I mean, we could have worked harder if we'd known that there was a reason to get done on time."

"Okay, class, it's time to put your relief maps on the back table to dry. As you all know by now, Meesha's group finished its map first, so that group has earned the free time I promised." The class politely claps for Meesha's group.

"Ms. Wyatt, we didn't get our map done," Molly calls out.

"That's 'cause you guys were too busy gossiping," Samantha teases. The class laughs.

"Samantha, it's not nice to tease your classmates," Ms. Wyatt says firmly, then turns to the three procrastinators. "But girls, I'm not particularly sympathetic. When I give you an assignment, I expect you to do it. I want the three of you to stay here until you finish it."

"But we'll miss music," whines Helen.

"You should have thought about that before you decided to goof off during your group time."

"But Derek and Nicholas got extra time to finish their work this morning," Molly points out.

"Yeah, it isn't fair if they get extra time to complete their work and we don't," Helen adds.

"I don't have any extra time to give you," counters Ms. Wyatt.

"Then why does Meesha's group get extra free time at the end of the day?" asks Lori.

"Enough," states Ms. Wyatt emphatically. "The rest of you line up for music."

Molly, Helen, and Lori are just finishing their relief map as their classmates return from music class. As soon as all her students have settled in their seats, Ms. Wyatt assigns two pages of division problems. "You have 20 minutes to complete these problems before the final bell rings," she announces.

"Ms. Wyatt?" Meesha asks. "What about the free time our group earned earlier? The rule is that free time must be used the same day we earn it. If we don't use it now, then we'll lose it."

"If you want to take the problems home and do them, you certainly can. Otherwise, you should do them in class during your free time."

"How is it free time if we still have to do work?" Meesha persists.

"Meesha, there's only so much time in a day. You can do the problems at home or at school, but you still have to do the problems."

"Last week you let Mary skip an assignment when she earned free time," Meesha reminds her.

"That was *last* week," Ms. Wyatt replies. "I'm sorry that you feel cheated, but you *do* have a choice here. We have a math test scheduled for tomorrow, and some of you need the extra practice with your long division. If you want to waste class time whining, that's your choice, too."

Possible questions for "Consequences":

1. *What inconsistencies do you see in how Ms. Wyatt responds to her students' behavior?*

2. *What might be Ms. Wyatt's rationale for offering free time to the group that finishes its map first?*

3. *Is the free-time incentive an effective one?*

4. *Vicarious reinforcement occurs when individuals increase the frequency of a response after they observe another person being reinforced for the same response. On what occasions might Ms. Wyatt be vicariously reinforcing her students?*

5. *From the perspective of social learning theory, how does Ms. Wyatt punish Meesha's group?*

6. *Ms. Wyatt doesn't allow Molly's group to attend music class. What message might this action send about music?*

7. *Ms. Wyatt teases Nicholas and Derek about their budding interest in the opposite sex. Is it appropriate for teachers to tease students in this way? Why or why not?*

8. *How might Ms. Wyatt's inconsistent behavior be affecting the overall psychological climate of the classroom?*

CASE 25
First Aid

The students in Mr. Mandabach's ninth-grade health class seem to be more hyperactive than usual this morning. Mr. Mandabach loudly clears his throat as a way of getting their attention. "All right, class," he says, "let's get started." He pauses until everyone has settled down. Out of the corner of his eye, he sees Ruth and Marisa quickly exchanging notes.

"As you know, we've been studying first aid procedures for a couple of weeks now. Today we're going to learn how we can help someone who has been in a serious accident." As Mr. Mandabach is speaking, he sees Paul pass a note to JoAnn.

Suddenly Mr. Mandabach remembers that the spring dance is coming up in a few days. Based on his five years' experience at Montview High School, he expects that the frequency of note-passing among his young adolescents will increase considerably between now and then. In his first year of teaching at Montview, he had always confiscated any notes that he saw and kept the culprits after class. But he eventually stopped doing it after a girl burst into tears as he read her note aloud to the others. So today he simply ignores any note passing he sees and continues with his lesson.

"Now imagine that you're all by yourself and come across an accident victim who is obviously unconscious. What do you think you should check first—breathing, airway, or circulation?"

"Airway," says Marie. Behind Marie, Juanita is shoving a note under Vicki's textbook.

"No, circulation," says Gary, "because people can bleed to death in a matter of minutes."

"It's breathing! " Ryan shouts. "If people don't get enough oxygen to their brains, they can become mentally retarded. People can even *die* if they don't get enough oxygen. Right, Mr. M.?"

"Yes," Mr. Mandabach agrees, "as you know, people can die if they go without oxygen for very long. Even if they *don't* die, they may suffer permanent brain damage."

"See, I told you, man! " exclaims Ryan.

"But now imagine this situation," Mr. Mandabach says. "A woman is eating a donut while she's driving to work one day. To help wash down the donut, she reaches for a can of Coke that's sitting in a cup holder next to her. As she does so, she takes her eyes off the road for a split second and crashes her car into a tree. She's not wearing a seat belt, so she's thrown 50 feet from the vehicle. You're riding your bike to school when you see the accident, and so you rush over to see what you can do to help. The woman is unconscious, and you see blood seeping from under her shirt. What should you do?"

"I'd call 911 on her car phone and wait for help to arrive," Greg replies.

"I'd lecture her about her poor eating habits!" Malcolm jokes.

Mr. Mandabach is pleased to see that all eyes are on him and the note passing has finally stopped. He repeats his question. "What would you *really* do to help?"

"Well, I'd look under her shirt to see where the blood is coming from," says Melody. "If she's bleeding a whole lot, then I'd apply pressure to the wound with my hand. I'd put my jacket between the wound and my hand, though, so I wouldn't get any of her blood on me."

"That's a good suggestion, Melody." Mr. Mandabach replies. "But how do you know if she's breathing? Maybe the bleeding is really a very minor problem compared to other things that are wrong."

Samantha raises her hand, and Mr. Mandabach nods his permission for her to speak. "Put your ear by her mouth and nose to see if you can feel her breath. Look at her chest so you can tell if it's rising or not."

"Aha! " Mr. Mandabach responds. "So what do you do if you see that she's *not* breathing? Think about what we did with the mannequins last week when the person from the Red Cross came to visit."

"Do CPR! " yells most of the class.

"Wait a minute," says Marie. "How do we know she's not choking on the donut? Maybe it's blocking her airway."

Mr. Mandabach looks around the room for reactions to Marie's observation, but there are none. "This time we *know* the person was eating prior to the accident. But most of the time, we aren't so lucky. We may not have a clue about what's going on when we first see an injured person. We should always check an unconscious person's *airway* first. Why do you think we should do this?"

"Because if we did CPR and her airway was blocked, we wouldn't be doing her any good," Gary replies.

"Right! You wouldn't be able to get any oxygen to her lungs no matter what you did. But now say that her airway *isn't* blocked. What would you do then?"

"You'd give her CPR," Malcolm answers.

"Right again," says Mr. Mandabach. *"So...airway, breathing,* and then what?"

"Circulation," Greg says.

"Good," says Mr. Mandabach. "We treat someone's bleeding...we deal with *circulation* problems...only after we've already made sure that he or she is breathing."

"Mr. M.?" asks Alisa. "What if we're all stressed out and can't remember which one comes first?"

"You have a point, Alisa," Mr. Mandabach responds. "But fortunately someone from the Red Cross came up with a very simple way to remember the order of first aid responses: *'A, B, C,'* for *airway, breathing, circulation.*"

"That's pretty clever the way you used 'A B C,' Mr. M." Blake tells him.

"Isn't it, though? Okay, let's consider another situation...."

NOTE: Every year, Mr. Mandabach made sure that his students became certified by the Red Cross in both First Aid and CPR.

Possible questions for "First Aid":

1. *What would you do if students were passing notes during a lesson?*
2. *How does Mr. Mandabach finally focus his students' attention on the topic of first aid?*
3. *Higher-level questions require learners to analyze, apply, or elaborate on new information. Lower-level questions require learners to report isolated facts in relatively the same fashion in which they learned the material. What types of questions does Mr. Mandabach ask?*
4. *Retrieval cues are hints that help learners recall information from their long-term memory. On what two occasions does Mr. Mandabach give his students retrieval cues to help them remember things they've already learned?*
5. *What evidence do we see that students are constructing new responses to Mr. Mandabach's questions rather than simply retrieving them from memory?*
6. *How frequently does Mr. Mandabach give his students feedback regarding the things they are saying?*
7. *From Piaget's perspective, at what stage of cognitive development must students be in order to understand first aid procedures?*
8. *From Vygotsky's perspective, the Zone of Proximal Development (ZPD) is the range of tasks that a student can perform only with the assistance of a more capable individual. How does Mr. Mandabach teach within his students' ZPD?*

CASE 26
The Respiratory System

Ms. McNaught has recently acquired some computer software that she can use to teach human anatomy and physiology to her high school biology students. The software depicts three-dimensional models of the human body that simulate such physiological phenomena as circulation, respiration, and digestion. The software also allows students to explore the models in a variety of ways—for example, by rotating or magnifying them, isolating particular systems or organs for closer inspection, or running simulations on specific systems.

Today, Ms. McNaught's students are in the computer lab using the new software to examine the "in's and out's" of human respiration. Sitting in pairs at various computer terminals around the room, the students have been instructed to identify the various components of the respiratory system, determine the function of each component, and explain how everything works in harmony to make respiration possible. Ms. McNaught gives each pair of students a worksheet on which to record observations and answer specific questions and then moves around the room to monitor students' progress and provide assistance where necessary. As she circulates, she hears snippets of several conversations.

Beau, a computer wiz, is the first student to bring a model of the respiratory system up on the computer screen. "Okay, Joan," he instructs his partner, "list these parts of the respiratory system: trachea, lungs, bronchi, bronchiole." He points to each part of the model as he names it, and Joan dutifully records the terms on the worksheet. Then Beau moves the mouse and clicks on another part of the screen. "Now let's see if we can make this guy breathe...."

As Ms. McNaught moves away from Beau and Joan, she overhears what Russell is saying to his partner Sally. "Put the names of the lobes here. No, not down there. Look at the computer model. This here is the middle lobe. This part down here is called the lower lobe."

Sally erases what she's written and then writes "middle lobe" and "lower lobe" in the places where Russell has indicated.

"What does it say to do next?" Russell asks.

"Ah...let's see. Oh, now we're supposed to figure out what the diaphragm and the rib cage do during respiration."

From another direction, Ms. McNaught overhears Carol complaining to her partner Keith. "Quit moving the model so fast. Honestly, I have to tell you this every time we do labs together! You change what's on the computer screen so fast that I can't get everything down on the worksheet. Come on, stop playing around, and turn the screen a little bit so I can at least see some of it."

The following day, Ms. McNaught conducts a class discussion of the respiratory system. "So who can tell me...what do the diaphragm and the rib cage do when we breathe?"

"The diaphragm moves down and the rib cage moves out," Diana answers.

"That's right. The diaphragm is a dome-shaped muscle just below the lungs, and when we breathe, it tightens and moves downward. At the same time, the muscles between the ribs pull the rib cage upward and outward. Now which process are we talking about here—inhaling or exhaling?"

"Inhaling," Keith answers.

"Good. Can you explain why you know it's inhaling?"

"Well, the diaphragm flattens out, and the rib cage moves forward, so there's more room inside the chest, and so air can come in."

"Good job, Keith. So what happens when the air enters the chest?"

After referring to his notes, Mark answers, "Air goes through the trachea and then through the bronchioles and into the alveoli."

"What happens when the air gets to the alveoli, Mark?" Ms. McNaught asks.

"Well, the alveoli are surrounded by lots of little blood vessels. The oxygen in the air passes through the membranes between the alveoli and the blood vessels and then goes into the blood."

"Excellent. Now which muscle does most of the work when we breathe?"

"The diaphragm," Kathy responds.

"Right," says Ms. McNaught. "About how many times a minute does a typical adult inhale and exhale?"

"About 10 to 16 times," Oliver replies.

"Is that when we're resting or working hard, Oliver?"

"When we're resting," Martin responds. "It's faster when we're running or something."

"Very good! Okay, class, for your homework assignment this weekend, I'd like you to write a one-page essay describing how the respiratory system works in conjunction with the cardiovascular system. In doing so, I hope you'll begin to realize just what marvelous machines our bodies really are. Class dismissed."

Possible questions for "The Respiratory System":

1. *In what ways are the male and female students in Ms. McNaught's class having different educational experiences?*
2. *Under the circumstances, why are the male students likely to learn and remember more than the female students about how the human respiratory system works?*
3. *Like most teachers, Ms. McNaught probably has no idea that her female students are having a different educational experience than the males. As a teacher, how might you minimize gender bias in your classroom?*
4. *Ms. McNaught ignores the students' bickering during their laboratory time. Is this a good strategy? Why or why not?*

5. *How might a computer simulation facilitate students' ability to construct an understanding of physiological systems?*

6. *Do you think that computer software that provides models and simulations of real-life systems and events can reasonably replace actual physical objects in high school science courses?*

CASE 27
Coming Back to School

Wesley Karasov was a top student at West Hills High School until last year, when he sustained a serious head injury in a motorcycle accident. He has undergone months of rehabilitation since the accident, and his parents and rehabilitation therapists believe that he is now ready to return to school. Today, Wesley and his parents are meeting in the school conference room with Wesley's former teachers, Principal Rob Wiggins, and Ms. Gila Seaver, the school's special education teacher. As a group, they will decide on an appropriate placement for Wesley.

After welcoming everyone to the meeting, Principal Wiggins begins the discussion. "Frankly, I'm not sure that he is ready to come back to school at all. I have the report from the psychologist at the rehabilitation center, and it looks as if his test scores just aren't where they need to be, especially for someone in his senior year of high school. In my mind, the best option right now is a private tutor. The school district has an excellent tutor on its payroll, and she could work with him at home for a couple of hours each afternoon."

As Wesley clears his throat to speak, all eyes turn to look at him. "My name is Wesley," he says in a slow, faltering voice. "I would appreciate it if you call me by my name. I am a person, not some object. It's my senior year, and I want to come back to school." Principal Wiggin's face turns beet red.

Wesley's mother, Mrs. Karasov, steps in. "Principal Wiggins, I'd like to remind you that Wesley has had a traumatic brain injury (TBI), something that entitles him to an appropriate education in the least restrictive environment possible. All three of us—Wesley, my husband, and I—have thought and talked a great deal about Wesley's situation, and we all believe quite strongly that his academic needs *can* be met in a regular high school environment. Since the accident, I've learned a lot about traumatic brain injuries. For instance, I've learned that people with TBI sometimes have rapid, and often quite sudden, improvements in mental capacity. These people need stimulation, and they need to be challenged."

"If Wesley were to come back to school right now, he'd probably have to spend most of the day in my special education classroom," Ms. Seaver observes. "His test scores are way below grade level. For example, I saw in the psychologist's report that he's reading at a first-grade level now. How can he possibly keep up with his classmates if he can't read high school level textbooks?"

Mrs. Karasov bites her tongue as she tries to keep her temper. "You've been looking at the test scores on *timed* tests, Ms. Seaver. Kids with head injuries usually need more time than other kids to think about what they read. Besides, Wesley took those tests eight months ago. He's grown a lot—mentally, I mean—since then."

As Principal Wiggins opens her mouth to respond, Mr. Karasov enters the conversation. "With all due respect, Principal Wiggins and Ms. Seaver, I think you're both grossly underestimating what Wesley is capable of doing. If you don't mind, I'd like to try a little experiment. I borrowed one of your school's history textbooks from a friend of Wesley's, and I've brought it with me today." Handing the book to the principal, he continues, "Choose any chapter you like, Principal Wiggins. Then let's send Wesley to the library to read it while we continue our discussion. Is that okay with you, Wesley?"

"I'll do whatever it takes to get me back in school," Wesley responds.

Wesley's parents and the members of the school faculty are in a heated debate when Wesley returns to the conference room with the history book and several sheets of notes. Principal Wiggins asks Mr. Hermanowitz, Wesley's former history teacher, to quiz Wesley on the chapter's content. Occasionally referring to his notes, Wesley correctly answers every question that Mr. Hermanowitz asks him.

Principal Wiggins looks at her colleagues, and their agreement about the situation is clear. She turns to Wesley and smiles. "I guess we owe you an apology, Wesley. You definitely *are* ready to come back to school. What can we do to make your life easier here at West Hills High?"

"Well, ma'am," Wesley responds, "I get tired easily. Sometimes I need to take a nap during the day. I forget what to do if I don't write things down. And mostly, I just need more time than the other students...."

As he attends his classes each day, Wesley keeps meticulous notes about the assignments he needs to complete and the due date for each one; as a result, he's been far more diligent than many of his classmates in getting his work done. He takes all of his tests in a room near the main office so that he has time to think about each question carefully; when he spends so much time completing his tests that he's late to other classes, the school secretary sends a note along with him to explain his tardiness.

By the end of second period each day, Wesley is so exhausted that he takes a two-hour nap on a couch in the nurse's office, but he wakes up refreshed enough to attend two more classes in the afternoon. The only drawback to his routine is that he's had to drop two of the classes he needs to graduate.

Meanwhile, Wesley's teachers are so impressed with the young man's determination to succeed that they bend over backwards to *help* him succeed. Aware of his difficulties in processing information quickly and in remembering what he's read and heard, they make a variety of accommodations on his behalf. For example, Wesley's mathematics teacher assigns him only half of the in-class exercises that she assigns the rest of the class; she asks him to do the remaining exercises at his leisure at home. His English teacher always writes directions to assignments on the board and then states them orally as well. His history teacher signals main ideas by saying, "This is important, so put it in your notes."

Ms. Struthers, Wesley's French teacher, is the most accommodating of all. Although Wesley had three years of French prior to his accident, he remembers very little of what he used to know so well. Although he's officially enrolled in French IV, Ms. Struthers teaches him out of the French I textbook. She encourages Wesley to speak in French in class, but she's patient when he struggles, and she occasionally gives him a word he needs if he has difficulty remembering it on his own. And whenever she gives her class a quiz, Wesley takes a French I quiz instead.

In a follow-up meeting, Wesley expresses his gratitude that the teachers are being so helpful and supportive. Other than having to give up his third- and fourth-hour classes, he thinks he has made a smooth transition back to school. Ms. Wiggins notes that all of Wesley's teachers are pleased with his progress.

NOTE: Wesley earned A's in everything except French that semester; however, he finished two courses shy of the school's graduation requirements. The school allowed him to attend his class's graduation ceremony in May but did not award him a diploma until August, after he had completed the missing courses in summer school.

Possible questions for "Coming Back to School":

1. *What accommodations did school personnel make for Wesley's disability?*
2. *If you had Wesley in your classroom, what other strategies might you use to help him succeed?*
3. *Zone Proximal Development (ZPD) is the range of tasks that a student can perform only with the assistance of a more capable individual. What strategies does the French teacher, Ms. Struthers, use to make sure that Wesley is working within his ZPD?*
4. *Should Wesley be officially enrolled in French IV? Why or why not?*
5. *What mistakes do Principal Wiggins and Ms. Seaver make when they interpret the test scores that the psychologist has reported?*
6. *Under the circumstances, should the school waive some of the graduation requirements in Wesley's case? Why or why not?*

CASE 28
The Concept Maps

Seventeen-year-old Robin is determined to be ready if her teacher, Mr. Kessinger, calls on her during her third-period world history class. Last night, she prepared a concept map—a diagram that depicts important interrelationships among the concepts in a chapter or unit—to help her remember the events that eventually led the United States into joining the Allied Forces during World War II. Now she has her concept map lying in front of her on her desk. As Mr. Kessinger fires questions at his students, Robin writes her classmates' responses in her notebook.

"So, Jacob, why didn't the United States jump in and help the Europeans when World War II began?"

"Well, at the beginning of the war, we thought the people in Europe should handle their own battles. When we first heard about how Hitler was having lots of Jewish people killed, we didn't believe that anybody could do such a thing. We thought all the stories were just lies that the media made up."

"Micki, when did we finally realize that there were many concentration camps all over Europe?"

"Uh...I'm not sure exactly," Micki answers hesitantly.

"Well, you should be!" Mr. Kessinger admonishes the girl angrily.

Micki squirms in her seat, then attempts to answer her teacher's question. "Well...when people...um...when European news reporters started sending us pictures of how horrible the war was, then we started getting involved. We...um...."

"I think that starting tonight, Micki, you'd better read your history book a little more carefully. Robin, exactly *what* event brought the United States into World War II?"

Taking a look at her concept map, Robin begins, "It was...." But then she sees Mr. Kessinger towering over her desk.

"What??!! You're using *notes*??!!" he screams as he tears her concept map into shreds.

As she watches the pieces of paper fall to the floor, she thinks to herself, "I worked for more than an hour on that concept map. Kessinger had no right to tear it up." Her teacher is saying something to her, but she doesn't hear him.

"Well, Robin? I'm waiting for an answer! What gives you the right to cheat in my class?!!" The rest of the class is quiet; everyone is too stunned to speak.

"I...I didn't think I was cheating," Robin stammers. "It's not as if this was a test. I thought I was supposed to be in here to learn. My concept maps help me connect different ideas together."

"You are expected to know this stuff before you come to my class. If you ever pull such garbage again, I will insist that you drop my class. Do I make myself *clear*?!"

Robin doesn't answer. And she doesn't look up from her desk until the bell rings. Her notebook remains open in front of her, but she writes nothing else in it for the rest of the class period.

Later in the day, as Robin is walking down the hall to Ms. Yamashita's psychology class, Jane and Cami run to catch up with her.

"Hey, are you okay, Robin?" Jane asks her. "I can't believe what Old Man Kessinger did to you today."

"I just hate him, I really do," Cami adds. "I mean, who cares if we take notes?"

As the three friends continue complaining about their world history teacher, they hear the bell ring. They hurry to their psychology class, arriving after class has already begun. Robin slips into her seat in the front row, pulls her psychology notebook out of her backpack, and opens it to the notes she wrote from her assigned readings the night before.

"Nice of you girls to join us," Ms. Yamashita says, smiling. "We're talking about Freud. Robin, what did Freud mean when he talked about the *id*?"

"The *id* is...uh...." As Robin pauses, she looks down at her notebook and realizes that the concept map she drew of Freud's theory is in full view of her teacher. Before she has a chance to hide it, Ms. Yamashita is at her desk and looking at her work. Robin cringes, expecting the worst.

"Why, Robin! This is lovely! Do you mind if I copy it for everyone else? Class, you should see this beautiful concept map that Robin has created...."

Oblivious to what her teacher is saying, Robin jumps quickly out of her seat and runs down the hall to the restroom, crying and shaking uncontrollably.

NOTE: Robin never again took notes of any kind in Mr. Kessinger's class. And even to this day, as a student in a doctoral program in educational psychology, she no longer creates concept maps. Mr. Kessinger received tenure many years ago and is still teaching as this case book goes to press.

Possible questions for "The Concept Maps":

1. *Explain Robin's reaction in Ms. Yamashita's class from the perspective of classical conditioning.*
2. *What possible advantages do concept maps serve?*
3. *Punishment I involves presenting a new stimulus that one perceives as unpleasant. Punishment II involves the removal of an existing stimulus that one finds desirable. What form of punishment did Mr. Kessinger practice on Robin?*

CASE 29
The Star Chart

Mr. Collins doesn't use basal readers or workbooks to teach reading to his second graders. Instead, he expects his students to read at least one book a week and write a description of what they've read. Students may choose their books from a wide assortment on the bookshelves at the back of the room. Each book is color-coded to indicate how easy or difficult it is; for example, books with yellow are very easy, and books with red dots are quite challenging.

Once the children have completed their reading requirements each week, they stick a gold star beside their name on the star chart at the front of the room. The child with the most stars at the end of the month will, for an entire week, have the first spot in line whenever the class goes somewhere; that child will also read his or her favorite book to the class.

On the last day of September, Mr. Collins announces the first "reading winner" of the school year: Courtney has earned seventeen gold stars, more than anyone else. The following morning, Mr. Collins asks Courtney to sit at the front of the room to read her favorite book. She has chosen Margret and H. A. Rey's *Curious George Goes Camping*, which is now lying open on her lap.

Courtney's voice begins to tremble as she stutters, "Je..Je..George an..and his f..f..friend...." She suddenly stops reading and looks to her teacher for assistance.

"You're doing fine, Courtney," Mr. Collins tells her. "Just slow down and have fun being the center of attention."

Courtney nods obligingly. "Je..Je..Je..George an..an..and his...I just can't do this, Mr. Collins."

"All right, Courtney, take a deep breath and relax. You've read this book at least a dozen times before."

"I guess I don't like bein' the center of attention," she replies. "I don't think that I can read this book in front of the class."

Mr. Collins kneels down to Courtney's eye level. "Does it scare you to read in front of the other kids?" he asks softly.

"Only when I'm reading up here in front of everyone," she whispers.

"You're such a lovely reader, but for some reason you're stuttering today. I wonder why."

She looks down ashamedly as she replies, "I'm afraid of messin' up."

Continuing to look at Courtney, Mr. Collins stands up, then speaks loudly so the class can hear what he has to say. "Maybe it will help you to know that you're among friends. Every one of us messes up from time to time. After all, we're only human." Courtney looks at the other children, who seem to be nodding their heads in agreement.

"Reading should be fun, not something scary," Mr. Collins continues. Let's first have you tell the class why this is your favorite book and what it's about, then the two of us can read your book together."

Courtney takes a deep breath and says, "Well...I love Curious George because he's fun and sweet, kind of like my baby brother. In this story, Curious George goes camping...."

NOTE: Courtney read five books a month the rest of the school year. She never earned "reading winner" again.

Possible questions for "The Star Chart":

1. *Is Mr. Collins's star chart a good idea? Why or why not?*
2. *Mr. Collins is trying to motivate his students to read by giving them gold stars for each book that they've read and then awarding special privileges to the student who reads the greatest number of books each month. For which children is this approach likely to be motivating?*
3. *For which children is Mr. Collins's approach unlikely to be motivating?*
4. *Do you think Mr. Collins is wise to let his students make their own choices about what they read?*
5. *State anxiety is a temporary feeling of anxiety that occurs during a threatening situation. Trait anxiety is a pattern of responding with anxiety even in non-threatening situations. What type of anxiety does Courtney exhibit?*

CASE 30
The Bulletin Board

As his third graders are working in pairs proofreading one another's short stories, Mr. Wilson begins to tack some of his students' spelling, mathematics, and social studies papers on the "Look What I Did" bulletin board. As he thumbs through the stack of papers in front of him, he notices a frown on Jordan's face. "What's the matter, Jordan?" he asks.

"My sister says I won't get any stickers next year 'cause I'll be in fourth grade. She says I'll be too old for stickers then. Is that true, Mr. Wilson?"

Kneeling down to be at Jordan's eye level, Mr. Wilson replies, "Well, that probably depends on who your teacher is. I know some fourth-grade teachers who give stickers and I know others who don't. Why do you ask?"

"Well, I'm in the third grade already, and I've *never* gotten a sticker on one of my papers, so I never get anything put up on the bulletin board. I was sorta hoping I might get one some day so's I could have my paper hung up."

"Don't feel bad Jordan, I've never had a paper hung up, either," Emma points out.

"Me, neither," adds Xias. "No matter how hard I try, I'm just not good enough for the bulletin board."

Mr. Wilson is dumbfounded. He's never realized that he has consistently excluded some children from his exhibits. "But, hey," he responds aloud, "it's only February. We still have lots of time for improving our study habits." He notices that the entire class is listening to the conversation.

Jordan looks frustrated as he replies. "I *always* make mistakes on my stuff, even though I don't mean to. Look," he says as he points to the papers on the bulletin board, "all of these have stickers. All of them! And do you notice something else? They all have A's on them!"

"Yeah," Xias agrees. "See...Tonya, A in math. Edwin, A in reading. Olga, A in math. Brad, A in history. Tori, A+ in science...."

Mr. Wilson looks more closely at the papers he's posted. "You know what? You guys are right. I was discriminating against some of you, and I didn't even know it. I think we'd better fix this situation right away."

"All right!" shouts Jordan. "So how are we gonna fix it?"

"Well, this bulletin board belongs to you—my students—not to me. How about if everybody brings me what you think is your best work—one paper for each of you—and we'll display it? And if you don't want to participate, that's okay, too." Mr. Wilson notices many of his students grinning as they rummage through their desks.

"Can we change what's up there once a week?" Emma asks.

"That's a great idea, Emma. Starting today, *you* choose what you want to go on *your* bulletin board and after lunch I'll put them up while you're at recess. Hmmm...I guess I'd better take down the things that are up here now and pass them back to their owners."

As he does so, Mr. Wilson tells himself, "And from now on, any child who shows improvement receives a sticker and a note saying 'Good progress'!"

Possible questions for "The Bulletin Board":

1. *What do you think is Mr. Wilson's rationale for posting good papers on the bulletin board?*

2. *What problems do you see in Mr. Wilson's practice of posting good papers on the bulletin board?*

3. *Self-efficacy is one's belief that one can perform a specific task successfully. How do you think the original bulletin board (i.e., the one that displays only the A papers) affects students' self-efficacy?*

4. *To what does Mr. Wilson attribute some students' consistently poor performance? Is his attribution an accurate one?*

5. *Is it appropriate for Mr. Wilson to give stickers when his students show progress, even if their performance is only marginally satisfactory?*

6. *A learning goal is a desire to obtain new information or skills; a performance goal is a desire to be judged favorably for one's achievement by one's peers. Does the bulletin board promote learning goals or performance goals? Justify your response with example(s) from the case study.*

CASE 31
Getting a Drink

Dari feels uncomfortable as she makes the seemingly endless trip from her desk to the drinking fountain at the back of the room. If she had a choice, she wouldn't make the trip at all. She is well aware that her classmates resent her being allowed to get a drink whenever she wants to, whereas they have to wait until recess or lunch. They know that the medicine she takes every morning makes her thirsty, but they still tease her about being the "teacher's pet."

"Why can't the others get drinks when they want to?" she wonders. "It wouldn't be any big deal. Besides, Ms. Patterson is *always* drinking her coffee. She carries that stupid coffee mug around so much that it looks as if it's attached to her body."

"Hey, Ms. Patterson, can I get a drink?" Craig calls out. "It's a really hot day, and I'm thirsty."

"Of course not, Craig. You know my rule about that." Ms. Patterson is obviously annoyed at his question.

Craig persists. "It's not fair. *You* can drink your coffee whenever you want to."

"I never said life is fair," Ms. Patterson replies. "I'm the teacher, so I have certain privileges. I need to have something to drink because I do most of the talking and my mouth gets dry. Besides, my job is to make sure that you children learn, and I can't do that if you're running to the drinking fountain all the time. It won't kill you to wait until recess to get a drink."

"But we could use a water bottle," Huong suggests.

"No, that won't work. A couple of years ago, I let my students bring water bottles to school, and they used them to squirt one another all the time. When are you people going to learn that no means no?"

"But you let Dari go to the fountain whenever she wants to," Shelby points out.

"Dari has medical problems," Ms. Patterson responds. "Anyway, I know that she'll only get a drink if she really, really needs one. Right, Dari?"

Dari nods self-consciously and then tries to make herself smaller by scrunching low in her seat.

"Yeah, she's special, all right," Guy scoffs. "She's the teacher's pet."

NOTE: This was Ms. Patterson's last year in the classroom.

Possible questions for "Getting a Drink":

1.   *From the perspective of Maslow's hierarchy of needs, what student needs may not be being met in Ms. Patterson's classroom?*

2. *Some motivation theorists propose that two conditions are essential for intrinsic motivation: self-efficacy (a.k.a., a sense of competence) and a sense of self-determination (a belief that one can control the course of one's life). With these conditions in mind, decide whether Ms. Patterson is promoting intrinsic motivation to behave appropriately in her classroom.*

3. *Ms. Patterson continually drinks coffee in front of her students. Is this appropriate? Why or why not?*

4. *Many students have a need for affiliation—a need to seek and maintain friendly relationships with others. What strategies might a teacher use to help Dari meet her need for affiliation?*

5. *State anxiety is a temporary feeling of anxiety which occurs during a threatening situation. Trait anxiety is a pattern of responding with anxiety even in nonthreatening situations. What type of anxiety did Dari demonstrate when she got a drink?*

CASE 32
Math Baseball

The students in Mr. Balcom's sixth-grade mathematics class have counted off by twos as a way of dividing themselves into two teams for a game of math baseball. The "Red Sox" have gone to the right side of the room, and the "White Sox" have gone to the left side. Each team is now lined up behind a strip of masking tape on the floor.

The students watch as Mr. Balcom draws miniature baseball diamonds on both ends of the chalkboard and attaches a small, magnetic picture of a baseball player at each "home plate." He then writes the same math problem just below the two diamonds he's drawn. As he places his piece of chalk in the chalk tray, he shouts, "Go!"

The two students at the front of each line—Tyrell and Corey—race to the board. Tyrell, who is playing for the Red Sox, solves the problem first. Because he's earned a "hit" for his team, he moves his team's baseball player to "first base." Corey is still struggling with the problem, but he knows that Mr. Balcom won't let him leave the board until he solves it correctly.

"I can't believe you haven't figured it out yet, Corey," Mr. Balcom admonishes him. "Come on, you can do this. Here, look at the way Tyrell did it.... Never mind, don't get so upset. It's only the first out for your team. There's still plenty of time to make runs."

Corey hears the other White Sox players moan. He marks an out for his team on the board and then walks slowly to the end of his line. A couple of his teammates pat him on the back as he walks by, but others are less kind.

"Thanks a lot for nothing, Corey."

"I can't believe you missed such an easy problem."

"Are you stupid or somethin'?"

As the game continues, Corey's mind is more on the clock than on the game. The minutes are ticking by ever so slowly. As the other team members have their turn "at bat," Corey moves closer and closer to the front of the line, and he soon finds himself standing right behind the masking tape once again.

"One more out and we lose the game," Chip whispers from behind him. "Come on, man, don't screw it up this time."

"I *hate* this game!" Corey thinks as he watches Mr. Balcom write the problem he knows he will have to solve.

"No goofing around this time, young man," Mr. Balcom warns as Corey approaches the board. "I expect you to show us what you know this time. Just think it through...."

NOTE: Corey was an extremely shy boy who didn't like being the center of attention. Although he had earned an A in math the preceding year, he earned an F in Mr. Balcom's class. His achievement in math slowly improved in the years that followed (e.g., a D the next year, and a C– the year after that), and he earned B's fairly consistently in high school.

Possible questions for "Math Baseball":

1. *What conditions are contributing to Corey's feelings of discomfort during the math baseball game?*
2. *Is the baseball game likely to help Corey improve his math skills?*
3. *To what extent is the baseball game likely to be motivating to the other students in the class?*
4. *Mr. Balcom says several things to Corey, presumably in an attempt to motivate him. Are his statements likely to be effective in this respect?*

CASE 33
The Perfectionist

Each time 13-year-old William begins a new drawing or painting in Mr. Mercurio's art class, he quickly becomes dissatisfied with his efforts and tosses what he has done into the wastepaper basket. After three months, he has yet to submit a completed project. Unless the situation changes, Mr. Mercurio realizes that he may have no choice but to give the boy a failing grade.

Hoping to curtail William's perfectionistic behavior, Mr. Mercurio scolds him for wasting art materials. Although William doesn't like being reprimanded, his wasteful behavior doesn't diminish; if anything, it's becoming more frequent. At wit's end, Mr. Mercurio finally keeps William after class one day to discuss the situation.

"Why does your work have to be perfect, William?"

"Because I don't want it to look stupid."

"I don't know of any art work that is 'stupid,' William, and I certainly don't know of any that is perfect. In my class, the most important things are to do your best and to work at improving your skills as the year progresses."

"But my best is never good enough. I'm not good at art. I don't want the other kids to see how bad I really am."

"I see. Well, then, why don't we try a different approach? Let's see if we can find today's project in the wastepaper basket. Ah, yes, here it is. How about finishing it at home tonight? You can bring it to me first thing tomorrow morning. That way, only you and I will see what you have done."

William reluctantly agrees and takes the crumpled paper that Mr. Mercurio is handing him.

At lunch time the following day, Mr. Mercurio finds William eating alone in the cafeteria and sits down beside him. "William, I waited for you this morning, but you didn't show up."

"I didn't have time to see you."

"Did you bring your art project to school?"

"No. I couldn't finish it last night because I had to do my chores."

"Do you think you will ever finish it?"

William hesitates. "Probably not."

"Why?"

"Because it looks ridiculous. Let's face it, I'm no artist."

Mr. Mercurio pulls out a small portfolio and spreads its contents on the table. "Here, let's look at some of your peer's artwork. Can you find one that's perfect?"

"This one is. Oh, it does have a few smudges. But these people can do a lot better work than I can. No matter how hard I try, I'm not any good at art stuff."

"Do you think these people were born knowing how to draw and paint, or did they learn how to do it with practice?"

"It seems to me that some people are just naturally better artists than others."

"So you think these people—the ones who did these pictures—don't have to put much effort into their work because they're born with artistic talent?"

"Of course they don't put much effort into it! They wouldn't be laughing and having fun during class if they had to try as hard as I do."

Mr. Mercurio looks William sternly in the eye. "Artistic talent comes from practice, not from heredity. You can only get better if you practice and then let me give you feedback."

Seeing no response from William, Mr. Mercurio stands up, then gathers the drawings and paintings he has brought and places them inside the portfolio. "You know, it's always the perfectionists who have trouble in my class," he says as he walks away.

NOTE: William committed suicide on his fifteenth birthday.

Possible questions for "The Perfectionist":

1. *A learning goal is a desire to obtain new information or skills; a performance goal is a desire to be judged favorably for one's achievement by one's peers. Does William have a learning goal or a performance goal in his art class?*

2. *Attribution is an individual's causal explanation for something that happens to the individual (e.g., a success or failure experience). To what does William attribute artistic performance?*

3. *If you were William's art teacher, what strategies might you use to help someone like William?*

4. *What evidence do we see that William may need to be referred to the school counselor?*

CASE 34
Cheerleading Tryouts

As Tina sits in Ms. Roche's first-period geometry class, she thinks about this afternoon's tryouts for the varsity cheerleading squad and smiles. There is no doubt in her mind that she will gain a position on the varsity squad. After all, she's one of the most popular girls at Grosvenor High School, and she's been captain of the junior varsity cheerleaders for the past two years.

Remembering that Ms. Roche has agreed to serve as coach for the varsity cheerleaders this year, Tina lingers after class to offer her assistance. "Say, Ms. Roche, I'll be glad to help you coach the new girls this year. I know all the cheers and everything, but some of the other girls are pretty clueless, you know."

"Why, thank you, Tina," Ms. Roche responds graciously. "I'll certainly keep your offer in mind."

Wearing her junior varsity captain's uniform from last year, Tina arrives at the gymnasium after tryouts have already begun. She sees several strangers sitting at a long table while Kara, a girl in her biology class, performs the routine she has planned. As the strangers observe Kara's performance, they occasionally make marks on the papers in front of them. A bit puzzled, Tina walks between the table and Kara, then plops herself down on the bleachers next to Sonya.

"Who are those people at the judges' table?" she asks Sonya.

"They're cheerleaders from State U.," replies Sonya. "Ms. Roche asked them to judge us this year so there wouldn't be so much bias in the ratings. Say, what's your tryout routine like?"

Ignoring her friend's question, Tina watches Kara and shrieks, "Get a load of those legs! Have you ever seen anything so *skinny*?" Overhearing her, Kara becomes flustered, and Tina snickers.

Ms. Roche, who has been standing on the sidelines, quickly approaches the bleachers. "Young lady!" she says sternly, looking directly at Tina. "You will keep your comments to yourself if you want to try out for a spot on my team!"

"Oh, I'm sorry," Tina responds sweetly. "I sure didn't mean to say that out loud." Then, turning to a group of students sitting behind her, she adds, "I think everyone should have an opportunity to try out, *even if she doesn't have a snowball's chance in hell of making it.*"

An hour later, Tina's name is called. Tina strolls over to the judges' table and introduces herself, then performs the same routine that she used during her junior varsity tryouts last year. "I've nailed it!" she thinks. "Ha! Didn't I look good in front of everyone!"

She looks at the judges, but they aren't smiling; in fact, two of them are shaking their heads in disgust. Tina senses that something is wrong. Maybe she shouldn't have walked in front of the table during Kara's routine.

"Is that all you're going to do for us today, Tina?" asks one of the judges. "Perhaps you didn't read the memo we sent to everyone last week. At this level, we expect to see splits, forward and backward flips, and walkovers."

Tina is too stunned to respond. After whispering with the others at the table, the same judge continues, "We'll let you have one more try. Give it your best shot this time."

"*Now*?" asks Tina in dismay. She notices that many of the students sitting in the bleachers, including Miss Skinny Legs, are clearly enjoying her obvious discomfort.

"Geez, I don't know how to do a back flip," Tina thinks. "I'll look like a complete fool in front of everyone." She repeats her routine with a hand stand and a forward flip, hoping that the judges won't notice that several required moves are missing. But they *do* notice, and Tina finds out later that afternoon that she hasn't made the squad.

The next day, Tina confronts Ms. Roche at the beginning of class. "It wasn't fair, you know. How was I supposed to know about the moves that were required for the tryout routine?"

"The requirements were listed in the school newspaper two weeks ago," Ms. Roche tells her. "They were also posted on bulletin boards throughout the school. And Ms. Bailey mentioned that there were new requirements at least three different times when she made her daily announcements over the intercom."

"It still wasn't fair. How was I supposed to change my routine in the middle of tryouts?"

Ms. Roche has little patience for Tina's unjustified fault-finding. "Maybe next time you'll pay closer attention to what you're supposed to do when you try out."

"Yeah, right! And what was the deal with those judges, anyway? You should have asked people from our own school, not a bunch of off-the-wall idiots!"

"Tina, we can discuss this after class. Now is the time for geometry."

"You're a real jerk, Ms. Roche! Too bad you're not a real *roach*, too, or I'd step on you." Tammy stomps to her seat. "What are *you* starin' at?" she yells at several of her classmates.

Ignoring Tina, Ms. Roche says, "Okay, class, before we begin today's group work, please hand in last night's homework assignment."

"I didn't have time to do it because I was wasting my time on some stupid, biased cheerleading tryout!" Tammy shouts. The entire class looks at Ms. Roche to see how she will respond.

"Class, it seems that Tina is having a bad day today. I think we had all better ignore her until she gets her temper under control." Tina leans back in her chair, crossing her arms and looking defiant.

Ms. Roche tries to draw the class's attention back to her agenda for the day. "Did anyone have trouble with the problems on the homework assignment?"

"I did!" Tina shouts. "But to tell you the truth, Ms. Roche, *you* are my biggest problem! What does a *roach* know about cheerleading anyway?!!"

"Tina, you have 60 seconds to get to the Counseling Office." When Tina hesitates, Ms. Roche screams, "*Now!*" Tina knocks several books and spiral notebooks off other students' desks as she storms out of the room.

"Roche is a jerk!" is Tina's parting shot as she disappears from sight. Ms. Roche is visibly shaken, but she proceeds with the day's lesson without further comment on what has just transpired.

NOTE: When Tina tried out for the cheerleading squad the following year and didn't make it, she and her parents tried to sue the school for "discrimination." She felt the school was biased against her "because she was aggressive." Her case was thrown out of court.

Possible questions for "Cheerleading Tryouts":

1. A learning goal is a desire to acquire new information or skills; a performance goal is a desire to be judged favorably for one's achievements by one's peers. Does Tina have learning goals or performance goals when trying out for the cheerleading squad? Justify your response with examples from the case study.
2. Attribution is an individual's causal explanation for something that happens to the individual (e.g., a success or failure experience). Characterize Tina's attributions regarding her failure to make the varsity cheerleading squad.
3. How does Ms. Roche respond to Tina's disruptive behaviors? Are her strategies effective?
4. Was it a good idea to send Tina to the office? Why or why not?
5. If you had a student like Tina, what strategies might you use to deal with her behavior?

CASE 35
Letters

After Ms. Bernstein's kindergartners arrive at their classroom the first thing Monday morning, they quickly put their backpacks and other items from home in their tote trays. They then go straight to the front of the room, find an empty spot on the painted red circle on the floor, and listen to the story that Ms. Bernstein is already starting to read aloud. School always begins with an exciting story, and the children don't want to miss it by squandering their time at their tote trays.

After she finishes the story, Ms. Bernstein sings hello to everyone by name to the tune of "Happy Birthday," like so:

> Good morning to Jack.
>
> Good morning to Jack.
>
> How are you this morning?

At this point, the child who's been identified in the song sings the final line:

> I'm fine, how are you?

The children are always delighted when they hear their own names called out in the song; their names are a signal they, too, can sing along with Ms. Bernstein. Once everyone has joined in, Ms. Bernstein brings the song to a close.

"Who *wasn't* in our song today?" she asks.

"Antonio wasn't in the song, Ms. Bernstein," Margaret calls out. "Remember? He has a doctor's appointment this morning."

"Denzel's not here, either," adds Justin. "He still has the flu."

Ms. Bernstein writes "Antonio" and "Denzel" on the chalkboard, sounding out each letter as she does so. "So...we have Antonio and Denzel absent today. Let's see, this week's office helper is Jon. Will you take this absentee form to the office for us, Jon?"

As Jon leaves the room, Ms. Bernstein begins a game of Riddly Riddly Ree, a game that the children know well. "Riddly, Riddly Ree, I see something you don't see. It has the colors of red, white, and blue. It begins with the letter *F*. What is it?"

"The fan!" responds Lena.

"Well, *fan* does begin with the letter *F*. But, let's look closely now. Is our fan red, white, and blue?" Ms. Bernstein asks.

"No, only white," Lena responds.

"That *car* over there!" Marcie volunteers, pointing to a toy car lying on top of the toy chest.

"Yes, Marcie, the car is red, white, and blue," Ms. Bernstein replies. "But it starts with a *ka* sound, doesn't it? What sound does *F* make?"

"Ef!" the class shouts.

"I know, it's *face*!" Tammy exclaims. "The clown's face is red, white, and blue!"

"No, it's *pink*, white, and blue," Mac points out.

"It's the *flag*!" yells Billy. "Our flag is red, white, and blue."

"Very good, Billy," Ms. Bernstein says. "Now it's *your* turn to have us guess something. Oh, welcome back, Jon. We're in the middle of a game of Riddly, Riddly Ree. Why don't you join us?"

"Riddly, Riddly Ree," chants Billy. "I see something you don't see. It has the color black. It begins with the letter *L*."

"The black *letters* on Josh's shirt?" Grant offers.

"Nope."

"The *little* black chair?" Tiffany asks.

"Nope."

"The black *lines* at the top of the bulletin board," Anamaria suggests.

"Nope."

"The black *lines* painted on the chalkboard where we practice our printing!" shouts Jane.

"Nope."

"How 'bout the black *Legos*—the ones someone tried to paint black with magic markers?" Mitch asks.

"No!" giggles Billy.

"We give up, Billy," Ms. Bernstein concedes. "What's black and begins with the letter *L*?"

"The *'lectric* cord on the end of the fan!" he answers smugly.

Ms. Bernstein smiles. "Ah, I see. You know, a lot of children pronounce the word that way. But actually, the word is 'electric,' like this." She writes the word in uppercase letters on the chalkboard. "See, it actually begins with the letter *E*. Okay, we didn't have a winner that time. Grant, why don't you think of the next word for us to guess?"

Ms. Bernstein eventually brings the Riddly Riddly Ree session to a close. "Boy, we had some really tricky ones today, didn't we? But fortunately, you are all really good guessers. It's always fun to think about the letters that different words start with, don't you agree, class?"

The children yell "Yes!" in unison.

"Today we will be making valentines for special people in our lives," Ms. Bernstein continues. The children clap and giggle with excitement as their teacher writes "VALENTINE" on the chalkboard. "What letter does the word *valentine* begin with?"

"*V*!" many of the children call out.

"Right! Let's have two volunteers make a *V* for us on the floor." Several hands shoot into the air. "Okay, Kelsie and Devin, come on up here and show us what the letter *V* looks like." Kelsie and Devin obligingly lie side by side on the floor next to where Ms. Bernstein is standing. The other children cluster around to watch.

Ms. Bernstein looks at Kelsie and Devin in mock puzzlement. "Hmmm, something's not right here, class. This doesn't look like a *V*, it looks more like two sticks beside each other." Kelsie and Devin giggle.

"They should put their feet together!" Julia suggests.

"Ah, good idea," Ms. Bernstein replies, as she stoops down to nudge Kelsie's and Devin's bodies into a *V*-like shape. "What do you think now, class? Do we have a *V*?"

"Yes!" the children answer.

"Good. But you know, we're going to be making a lot of valentines this morning, so one "*V*" isn't going to be enough. Each of you find a partner to make a valentine with on the floor." The children pair off and find empty spots around the classroom. Ms. Bernstein circulates to inspect the *V*s each pair made, occasionally teasing children who have made crooked ones.

"Well done, boys and girls," Ms. Bernstein commends her students. "Now let's all come back to the circle to talk about how we might want to make our valentine cards."

The children walk quickly back to the red painted circle at the front of the room. Once everyone is seated and looking attentively in her direction, Ms. Bernstein begins. "Let's think about the people we might want to make our valentines for. Hmmm...we could make one for our mother or our father. We could make one for a grandparent or an aunt or uncle. We could make one for a brother or sister. We could even make one for a friend or neighbor. But I'm curious...why do we make valentine cards anyway?"

"To show people that we love them," Wesley answers.

"To give them something pretty," says Kyong.

"To make them feel good," says Marnie.

"Yes," Ms. Bernstein replies, "a valentine can mean all of those things. Now, I realize that you all may have lots of special people in your lives, so if you finish your first valentine early, you can make another one. Somewhere on your valentine, I would like you to write a special note saying how much you care about the person you're going to be giving it to. When you write your note, try sounding out the words on your own. Write your message on a piece of scrap paper first, then I'll help you with your spelling. Remember, the word *valentine* is written on the board in case you want to use it in your message."

Noticing that Joshua is staring out the window, Ms. Bernstein gently puts her hand on his shoulder to regain his attention. "There isn't any right or wrong way to make a valentine. I brought in some examples of valentines that other students have made. Notice how different they all are. You can make your valentine any way you like. Now please listen closely to my instructions before you return to your seats. You should all walk *quietly* to your tote trays to get your pencils, crayons, scissors, and glue. Then walk *quietly* to your seats and begin to work. You'll find red, pink, and white construction paper on every table. Okay?" Ms. Bernstein pauses to be sure that all eyes are on her. "Then let's make valentines!"

The children chatter happily among themselves as they work on their valentines, but Ms. Bernstein doesn't seem to mind the noise. Instead, she walks around the room, helping the children with their written messages. She is not surprised to find many misspellings in what the children have written. For example, in large black letters, Sally has written "I LUV U MOME. WLL U BE MI VALENTINE." Underneath Sally's words, Ms. Bernstein prints in smaller letters, "I LOVE YOU, MOMMY. WILL YOU BE MY VALENTINE?"

"This is how the words are spelled in the printed world, like in our storybooks," Ms. Bernstein tells Sally. Then, continuing to circulate about the classroom, she shows the other children how each of their messages is spelled "in the printed world."

A half hour later, Ms. Bernstein rings a bell on her desk, and the children scramble to tidy up their tables. Several of them get a bit rowdy as they throw their discarded construction pieces into the recycle bins. Ms. Bernstein flicks the switch for the overhead lights on and off, and the room immediately becomes quiet. The children whisper to each other as they finish their cleanup and then head over to the red circle.

Ms. Bernstein smiles at her class. "I like how you used your 'indoor voices' to finish cleaning up your mess. My, aren't your tables spotless!"

Possible questions for "Letters":

1. *What classroom management strategies does Ms. Bernstein use to keep her students on task throughout the morning?*
2. *What strategies does Ms. Bernstein use to keep her children's attention throughout the morning?*
3. *In what ways does Ms. Bernstein take diversity in children's backgrounds into account?*
4. *Using the notion of knowledge construction, explain Billy's belief that "electric" begins with L.*
5. *How does Ms. Bernstein respond to Billy's erroneous belief that "electric" begins with the letter L?*
6. *Ms. Bernstein says, "Riddly, Riddly, Ree, I see something you don't see. It has the colors of red, white, and blue. It begins with the letter F. What is it?" Lena answers "fan," referring to a fan that is only white. How might you explain her error using the idea that working memory has limited capacity?*

CASE 36
Halloween

As her third graders head out the door at the end of one school day late in October, Ms. Gonzales hands each of them a letter to take home to their parents or guardians:

Dear Friends,

This coming Friday, we will celebrate Halloween with our traditional costume parade and class party. If your child does not have a costume but would like to participate in the parade, the school has a number of costumes available. Please call the school secretary, Mrs. Witherspoon, if you think your child might like to borrow one.

Our room helpers have been busily baking cupcakes and purchasing other party treats. We would certainly welcome additional contributions from those of you who have the time and energy to provide them. Because a few students in our class have either food allergies or diabetes, I would ask that you not send any items that include either *sugar* or *peanuts*. Might I suggest fruit, sugarless gum, or inexpensive plastic trinkets as items that the children might enjoy.

If you would like to help out at our party, I would certainly love to have you join us. The Halloween celebration here at Northrup Elementary is always fun for parents as well as children. Feel free to give me a call if you have any questions.

Sincerely,
Ms. Celeste Gonzales

Friday morning, most of Ms. Gonzales's second graders arrive with their costumes in their backpacks or in grocery bags. Although they are clearly excited about the afternoon's Halloween festivities, Ms. Gonzales tells them that it will be "business as usual" in her classroom until after lunch time. After taking attendance and collecting lunch money, Ms. Gonzales calls one of her reading groups to the reading table and instructs the other children to continue working on the math problems they began the day before.

Ms. Gonzales notices that her students seem considerably more distractible than usual this morning. The children in her reading group don't seem to be focusing on the story they are reading. Instead, they keep looking at the clock on the wall or exchanging meaningful glances with one another. A stern look from their teacher is usually enough to get them back on task, but rarely for very long.

Meanwhile, Ms. Gonzales is also keeping an eye on the other children in her classroom—those who are supposed to be working independently on their math assignment. Everyone is exceptionally fidgety today, and there is a great deal of whispering from one desk to another. Ms. Gonzales finds herself having to call out several children's names as a way of silencing them.

During recess, she looks over her students' math papers. The papers are messier than usual, and about half of the children didn't complete all the assigned problems. "I hope that recess will help them release some of their energy," she thinks. "Otherwise, it's going to be a *very* long morning."

After recess, Ms. Gonzales gives the weekly spelling test. All of the words this week are related to Halloween.

"Okay, class, now that you have your paper and pencils ready, let's begin. The first word is *Halloween*. Today we are having a *Halloween* party. *Halloween*." The children giggle, then write the word on their papers.

"Next word. *Pumpkin*. Today our class will carve a *pumpkin* during our party. *Pumpkin*."

"Are we really carving a pumpkin?" asks Tandy.

"Yes," Ms. Gonzales replies. The children clap and squirm in their seats.

"Word number three. *Party*. We will have a *party* only if you all calm down. *Party*." She smiles as the children try to sit more quietly in their seats.

NOTE: The following year and thereafter Ms. Gonzales provided group projects in the mornings before each party to allow the children to talk with one another without getting into trouble.

Possible questions for "Halloween":

1. *What are some classroom management techniques Ms. Gonzales implements prior to the Halloween celebration?*
2. *Should teachers try to teach academics on the day of a party?*
3. *Is it a good idea for Ms. Gonzales to focus the week's spelling list on words related to Halloween?*
4. *Some children and their parents choose to exclude themselves from any type of school party. How can you, the teacher, inform these individuals of an upcoming event without offending or ostracizing them?*

CASE 37
The Stand-up Comic

Although thirteen-year-old Connor arrives at Kennedy Middle School each day clean and well groomed, his threadbare clothes set him apart from the other students. After two months, he hasn't found a single friend—a single classmate who will accept him as he is.

Connor's impoverished circumstances are called to everyone's attention at the beginning of third-hour history class one day. When Mr. DeVenney is temporarily distracted by a message from the main office, Zach calls out, "Hey, Mikey, what's with wearin' the same two pairs of pants all the time? Haven't ya noticed that they're way too short for you and are, like, fallin' apart?"

"I can't help it if my family doesn't have much money," Connor replies sullenly.

"Like, how poor *are* you? I see you eatin' a peanut butter sandwich and drinkin' Koolaid everyday at lunch. Don't you know that they have free lunches for people like you? Maybe you'd get a little more variety." The other students are all looking in Connor's direction.

Connor is quiet for a moment, but his face suddenly lights up when he thinks of a witty come-back. "My family's so poor that we take a rolling pin to mash out a piece of bread, pour catsup on it, and call it pizza." Many of the students giggle at his joke, although a few seem to feel a bit awkward about doing so.

"Of course," he adds, "my brother puts on a newspaper hat, walks around the block a few times with the pizza in his hand, then rings the doorbell. Now we're really feeling all hotsy-totsy, 'cause we're gettin' home delivery!" The entire class bursts into laughter, and Mr. DeVenney looks up to see what is going on.

"It's sad, though," Connor continues. "Sometimes my brother forgets where we live, and then the pizza gets cold." By this time, the class is rolling in the aisles. Mr. DeVenney is not quite sure what has just happened, but he's pleased to see Connor finally interacting with his peers.

"Hey, Mikey," Zach calls out, "you're all right, dude." Connor is grinning from ear to ear.

"Okay, you two," Mr. DeVenney tells them warmly but sternly, "I think you've taken enough of our valuable time. Let's get started with today's lesson. As you should remember from yesterday, we've been talking about the Industrial Revolution...."

As he proceeds with his lesson plan, Mr. DeVenney has trouble keeping the class on task, because Connor, who's always been so quiet and well-behaved, *interjects I'm so poor...* jokes as often as he can think of them. The class responds more enthusiastically with each new joke, and Connor is obviously delighted by the attention.

"Oh, well," Mr. DeVenney thinks to himself, "What's wrong with not making any progress for one day? The kid's having his moment in the sun. It'll probably never happen again."

By the beginning of December, Mr. DeVenney has lost all control of his third-hour history class. Although Connor seems to have exhausted his supply of *I'm so poor...* jokes, he has developed a repertoire of jokes on virtually every other topic—school, sports, politics, religion, even the weather. Mr. DeVenney is at a loss for what to do. He has tried ignoring Connor, reprimanding him in front of his classmates, sending him to the office, keeping him after school, making him eat lunch in the teacher's lounge, sending notes home, and, on one occasion, meeting with his parents. Yet Connor's joke-telling continues unabated.

Exasperated after one especially rough day, Mr. DeVenney keeps Connor after class. "No matter what I do, you won't shut up," he admonishes his class clown. "Thanks to you, we've hardly accomplished *anything* in the last few weeks."

"I'm sorry," Connor replies a little sheepishly. "But you know, Mr. D., it feels good to be liked for a change."

Mr. DeVenney suddenly understands why Connor has been behaving as he has. "I see. Hmmm...." He pauses, rubbing his chin as he thinks the situation through. "Okay, then, I tell you what. I'll let you tell one joke at the very beginning of class each day. I'll even let you stand at the front of the room to tell it, like a stand-up comic would do. I have one condition, though—you cannot tell any jokes that degrade other human beings in any way. In other words, no religious, racial, ethnic, sexist, or sexual orientation put-downs. And remember, you can tell only *one* joke a day. What do you think?"

"How about two jokes?"

"One joke, and it has to be at the beginning of the period."

"It's a deal," Connor replies as he reaches out to shake Mr. DeVenney's hand.

After his second-hour class each day, Mr. DeVenney finds a chair at the back of the classroom so that Connor can have the "stage" to himself when he arrives at the beginning of third hour. Connor is never late to class, but he usually arrives just before the bell rings so that he can make a grand entrance. He tells his joke for the day, priding himself on his delivery and timing as much as on the joke itself. Despite his classmates' frequent encouragement for an encore, Connor keeps his word to Mr. DeVenney, limiting himself to a single joke and then taking his seat.

"This is working well," Mr. DeVenney concludes. "Once Connor finishes his joke, I seem to have my students' full attention for the rest of the hour. As a matter of fact, I can't think of any other time in my teaching career when I've had a class so completely under control."

Connor continues "performing" in his third-hour history class for several weeks. Then one day, he approaches Mr. DeVenney after school. "I...uh...I don't think I need to tell jokes anymore, Mr. D."

"Oh?"

"Well...I have friends now. I eat lunch with them and stuff. We do things together...well, things that don't cost money...and we hang out."

"And what does all this have to do with your jokes?"

"Well, my jokes gave me a chance to let the other kids get to know me, and I liked all the attention I was getting. But now that I have friends, I can get attention in other ways."

"That's a very insightful observation, Connor. I'm really proud of you."

"Well, thanks, Mr. D...thanks for everything."

"Damn!" Mr. DeVenney says to himself as Connor walks out the door. "I'm going to miss those jokes."

NOTE: Connor is now a successful chemical engineer. He has provided college scholarships to two boys residing at a homeless shelter where he volunteers his time every Saturday.

Possible questions for "The Stand-up Comic":

1. *Explain Connor's joke-telling behavior from the perspective of operant conditioning.*
2. *To what extent does Mr. DeVenney display withitness at the beginning of the case study?*
3. *Is Mr. DeVenney's strategy for addressing Connor's distracting influence an effective one? Why or why not?*
4. *What does Mr. DeVenney do to preserve Connor's self-esteem when he keeps the boy after class?*
5. *Would it have been better for Mr. DeVenney to let Connor tell his joke at the end of class rather than at the beginning? Why or why not?*
6. *If you discover that a student is being ostracized by his or her classmates, as Connor initially is, what might you do to help?*

CASE 38
Proofreading

When they arrive at their sophomore English composition class, Mr. Kalantari's students immediately copy into their notebooks the two sentences that the overhead projector is displaying on the wall:

- a stranger in an black suit knocked on my neighbors door and handed him a plane brown envelope
- connie my sister begined her paper route at 730 am and finish it at 845

Mr. Kalantari waits patiently for a few minutes while his students correct the two sentences for capitalization, punctuation, grammar, and spelling errors.

Then, poised at the front of the room with his red transparency marker in hand, Mr. Kalantari greets his class. "Good afternoon. It looks as if you've all made your editorial changes. Now tell me what mistakes you want me to fix in the first sentence."

"Capitalize the *a* before 'stranger'," Rafael tells him.

"Turn *'an* black suit' to *'a* black suit'," says Fern.

"Put an apostrophe between the *r* and *s* in 'neighbors'," says Koy.

"Why isn't the apostrophe *after* the *s* in 'neighbors'?" Mr. Kalantari asks.

When Koy hesitates, Katie replies, "'Cause you're only talking about one neighbor."

"Does anyone disagree with Katie about where the apostrophe should go in 'neighbors'?" He pauses for a few seconds and looks around the room, but no one seems to have any objections to Katie's explanation. " Are there any more mistakes in the first sentence?"

"Yeah," Pam responds. "The word 'plane' is spelled wrong. It should be p-l-a-i-n."

"Good! Anything else?" Mr. Kalantari asks. The students shake their heads. "Careful," he prods them, "there's one more mistake that you've missed here. I'll give you a hint: in addition to having a capital letter at the beginning of the sentence, there's also something we have to have at the *end* of the sentence."

The students laugh, and several of them shout, "A period!"

"Hey, I'm looking at a bright bunch of teenagers today. Okay, I think we've finally made the first sentence presentable. Now what about the second one?"

"Capitalize the *c* in 'connie,' and put a period at the end of the sentence," Bill suggests.

"Put commas around 'my sister'," says Graham.

"Why do we put commas around 'my sister'?" Ron asks.

"The words 'my sister' are an appositive phrase because they identify who Connie is," Graham responds.

"Put colons after '7' and '8,' and put periods after *a* and *m* in 'am'," Fern says.

"'Begined' isn't a word," adds Koy. "It should be 'began.' And 'finish' should be 'finished'."

"All of you did a fine job correcting today's sentences! Now remember to circle anything that you missed. Over a period of time, you might be able to see if there are any patterns to your errors."

"Mr. Kalantari, why do we have to correct sentences every time we come to class?" asks Clark.

"That's a good question, Clark. Does anyone have an answer?"

After a few seconds of awkward silence, Jamie raises her hand, and Mr. Kalantari nods for her to speak. "Well," she explains, "I think that correcting sentences every day helps me edit my own writing. Like, when I write my persuasive essays, I know that I have trouble with comma splices, so I watch out for them now."

"Yeah, it's nice to figure out my own mistakes instead of having a teacher point them out for me," adds Gary.

"Did that answer your question, Clark?" Mr. Kalantari asks. Clark mumbles something in affirmation. "Okay, then, let's move on to the autobiographical stories you've been working on. As I promised you yesterday, you can have 30 minutes to proofread one another's work. Help me out here—what are some key things you may want to watch out for?"

"Subject-verb agreement," Rafael offers.

"Make sure the verb tenses stay the same all the way through," Pam suggests.

"Look for places where you should have a comma or quotation marks," Ron adds.

"Okay, we've gotten some good ideas in terms of grammar and punctuation," Mr. Kalantari observes. "Now what should you be looking for in terms of the *content* of the essays you're proofreading?"

"We have to make sure that everything fits together," Kirk replies. "You know, what we write should be organized and logical and stuff like that."

Mr. Kalantari nods his head in agreement. "Good, Kirk. Now then, when you're reading someone else's story, what should you do if you don't know what the author is trying to communicate?"

"How about just writing a note saying what the problem is?" Lacy says. "Or maybe putting a question mark by the confusing parts?"

"Those are excellent suggestions, Lacy. All right, let's get started. Just like you did the last time, have at least two other students proofread your work. And this time, I'd like for you to use at least one proofreader that you haven't used before. The students who proof your papers should sign their names at the top of the first page, so I know who's read what. Any questions? Okay, then, find a proofreading partner and get started."

After giving his students a few minutes to get started on their proofreading task, Mr. Kalantari begins to circulate around the room to provide assistance where it might be needed. While he is helping George and Anton with the subject-verb agreement in George's story, he overhears Jamie and Marla talking about their after-school plans. As he continues working with the boys, he gently reaches over to tap

Jamie's desk. Out of the corner of his eye, he sees both Jamie and Marla get back to work.

After conferring with Renée about the correct order of quotation marks and a comma when they appear together in the middle of a sentence, Mr. Kalantari walks to the front of the room and writes a "2" on the chalkboard. Several of the students look up to see what he is doing, then return to their work. They know that the "2" indicates their teacher's rating of the current noise level in the classroom. On Mr. Kalantari's five-point "volume" scale, a rating between 1 and 3 is in the acceptable range.

Mr. Kalantari resumes his cycle around the classroom. As he walks by Gretchen, he notices that she is leaning backward on the two back legs of her chair. He gently touches her shoulder, and she immediately returns her chair to an upright position. "Thanks, Gretchen," he whispers.

Meanwhile, he hears Kathleen complaining to her partner, "Geez, Todd, what do *you* know about this stuff? Just sign your name and we'll call it even." Mr. Kalantari looks her in the eye, and she becomes quiet.

Mr. Kalantari asks, "Todd, what do you think of Kathleen's story?"

Todd hesitates, wondering how to be tactful. "Well, she has good grammar and spelling and stuff, but all she does is describe what people are *doing*. She needs to talk about what they're thinking and feeling, too."

"Hmmm...interesting observation. What suggestions do you have for Kathleen to help her out here?"

"Well, take this paragraph about her brother catching the fish. She could talk about how big the fish was. She could talk about how he felt to be fishing, or maybe how he felt catching such a puny fish in front of his friends."

"I think you've given Kathleen some good ideas about how she might strengthen her story, Todd," Mr. Kalantari says. "Don't forget to write your suggestions somewhere on her paper."

"Okay, class, please return to your own seats." Mr. Kalantari waits while his students get settled, then asks, "I'm curious, why do you think I have you proofread one another's papers?"

"Because sometimes you don't feel like doin' your job," Bill jokes.

Mr. Kalantari takes Bill's comment in stride, then asks his question in a different way. "What might *you* gain from reading someone else's work?"

No one seems to have an answer.

"Well, I'd like you to think about my question tonight." As the bell rings to signal the end of class, Mr. Kalantari has to raise his voice to be heard. "Remember, your final draft is due tomorrow. Don't forget to turn in your rough draft, too. Great job today. I think you all got a lot accomplished."

Possible questions for "Proofreading":

1.   *On what occasions does Mr. Kalantari use positive reinforcement?*

2.   *What strategies does Mr. Kalantari use to keep students on task?*
3.   *What strategies does Mr. Kalantari use to cue students about inappropriate behavior?*
4.   *Traditionally, the teacher is the one who evaluates students' performance in the classroom. Recently, a number of theorists have proposed that ultimately students must learn to evaluate their own performance. What strategies does Mr. Kalantari use to promote such self-evaluation?*

CASE 39
Horses and Aliens

This year, for the first time, Mr. Fredrickson has been assigning cooperative group projects in his fourth-grade class. Unfortunately, it seems as if his students have been using their group time more to socialize than to accomplish the tasks he's assigned.

"We seem to be having trouble getting work done in our cooperative groups," he tells his class one morning. "Before we meet in our groups today, I think we need to come up with some rules that might help us stay on task. Does anyone have any suggestions?"

"Talk softly," suggests Marguerite. "Sometimes this room is so noisy that I can't even hear what the other people in my group are saying."

"Thank you, Marguerite, that's a good start." Mr. Fredrickson writes "Cooperative Group Rules" at the top of the chalkboard, underlines it, then adds "Talk softly" immediately below.

"I think we shouldn't interrupt each other," Isaiah says. "It's like you said the other day, everyone has something to contribute. We don't interrupt when we're altogether in one big group, so why should we interrupt when we're in *small* groups?"

Mr. Fredrickson adds "Don't interrupt" to the list on the chalkboard.

"We all need to help one other," Kim offers. "It shouldn't always be the same people who are doing the helping."

"Everyone should contribute to the project," Mr. Fredrickson writes. Then he says, "That reminds me, in case you haven't noticed already, I've put at least two boys and two girls in each group. That means that sometimes boys will help girls and sometimes girls will help boys. I know that a few of you want to avoid members of the opposite sex at all costs." The children laugh. "But you know what? You just might learn something from them."

Mr. Fredrickson looks at the list he's created on the chalkboard. "Okay, we've established three rules for our cooperative groups. One, *talk softly*. Two, *don't interrupt*. And three, *everyone should contribute to the project*. Do these rules seem agreeable to all of you?"

"Yes," the children respond.

"So, then," Mr. Fredrickson continues, "let's talk about this afternoon's group project. I want each group to come up with a story that contains all 15 of our new spelling words. How do you think you might do this so that everyone in the group contributes?"

"We can make sure that everyone adds at least one sentence to the story," Emily proposes.

"Good idea, Emily. And how can you have everyone contribute when the group is writing its story down on paper?"

"How 'bout if we each write our own sentences in the story?" Marguerite asks hesitantly.

"Does Marguerite's suggestion make sense to the rest of you?" Hearing no objection, Mr. Fredrickson continues. "How do you think you should begin to write your stories? Do you just pass a sheet of paper from one person to another and each do your own thing?"

"No," laughs Cecily. "First we need to decide what we want to write about. Then we can write our sentences on strips of paper and lay them out on the table."

"Do you mean that you should put them in a sequential order so the story makes sense?" asks Mr. Fredrickson.

"Yeah, that's what I mean," Cecily replies.

Mr. Fredrickson nods in approval. "So then you can copy all of the sentences onto a single sheet. All right, children, it looks as if you know how to proceed, so it's time to assemble in your groups." Familiar with the routine, the students pull out pencils and sheets of notebook paper and then move their desks to form clusters of five.

Once the noise has subsided, Mr. Fredrickson announces, "Remember, folks, at the end of the first six weeks, you will receive both individual grades and group grades in spelling. How do you earn your individual grades?"

"The spelling tests on Fridays!" Lucas shouts out.

"Right. And how do you earn your group grades?"

Kim raises her hand. "Whenever we do group projects, everyone gets the same grade for it."

"Right, Kim. So then I'll take the two sets of points—your Friday quiz scores and your group points—and combine them into one spelling grade. Is there anything else special about cooperative group work?"

Charlie is the first to respond. "The group that has the most points at the end of the week gets ten minutes of free time!"

"Good memory, Charlie. Okay, you have 40 minutes to write your stories. I've listed the 15 spelling words on the board. Each one needs to appear in your stories at least once. Oh, yes, and be sure that you all remember to follow our new cooperative group rules."

"Let's write a story about horses," Kim suggests to her group.

"Writing about aliens from outer space would be more fun," counters Cecily. "Besides, *alien* is one of the spelling words."

"Yeah, aliens!" Bryan agrees. Bryan knows from past experience that Cecily will probably do his work for him, so it's not a bad idea to back her up.

"Horses is a better topic," Sean insists.

"What do you think, Robert?" Kim asks the fifth member of the group. "It should be horses, shouldn't it?"

Robert, who is terribly shy, just shrugs his shoulders and mumbles, "I don't care."

"You're being stupid!" Cecily tells Kim. "Who cares about horses? Have you ever even ridden one?"

"As a matter of fact, I *have*," Kim retorts. "Have *you* ever seen an *alien*?"

"I think they're interesting," Cecily responds. "You do, too, Robert, don't you?"

Robert says nothing.

"Why don't we write about horses next time?" Cecily suggests as a compromise. "Besides, we'll be working together all month. Let me have my idea first, then you can have yours next time."

"How can you be so selfish?" Kim replies. "There are other people in this group besides you. Isn't that right, Robert?"

Robert watches Mr. Fredrickson work with another group. He thinks about seeking his teacher's help to get the group on task but then decides against it.

"Okay, class, you've been working for ten minutes now," Mr. Fredrickson announces. "Your stories should be well under way, and each of you should have contributed at least one sentence by now."

"Don't be so stubborn!" Cecily admonishes Kim. "You know we'll all get zeroes if you don't help us write this alien story."

"Cecily," Kim says sternly, crossing her arms, "we'll get zeroes if *you* don't help with this story about *horses*."

Sean leaves the group and walks over to Mr. Fredrickson, "We're not gettin' anywhere. We need help."

Mr. Fredrickson approaches the group. "What seems to be the problem?" he asks.

"It's Cecily!" Kim shouts. "She won't do what we want."

"Yeah, right!" Cecily counters angrily. "Kim is the one who isn't cooperating. We haven't started writing our story yet, and it's all because of her."

"What are you writing about?" asks Mr. Fredrickson.

"Horses!" says Kim.

"Aliens," says Cecily. "Horses are a dumb idea."

"And aliens *aren't* dumb?" Kim asks pointedly.

"Hmmm...why not horses stuck in an alien world?" Mr. Fredrickson suggests.

The group readily agrees and buckles down to work.

Before group time the following day, Mr. Fredrickson says, "We need to add another rule to our cooperative group rules. Does anyone have any idea what it might be?"

"Not to put one another down," says Robert. This is the first time all year that Robert has volunteered to say anything in class.

Mr. Fredrickson smiles. "Hmmm," he thinks, "maybe these cooperative groups are teaching the children more than I realized."

Possible questions for "Horses and Aliens":

1. *Many fourth graders have trouble writing short stories. With this in mind, consider the benefits that a cooperative story writing task might have.*
2. *In what ways does Mr. Fredrickson try to follow generally recommended guidelines for facilitating productive cooperative groups?*
3. *How might a teacher keep "bossy" children such as Kim and Cecily from dominating group discussions?*
4. *Mr. Fredrickson creates competition by having the groups compete for free time—a reward that will be awarded to only one group. Is this a good idea? Why or why not?*
5. *What are some instructional objectives that Mr. Fredrickson might be trying to accomplish through the group story-writing activities?*

CASE 40
Endangered Species

Ms. Dennison's fifth-grade class will be spending the next six weeks studying endangered species in the western hemisphere. Ms. Dennison introduces the topic with a 25-minute videotape about manatees that live off the coast of Florida. The video depicts manatees' physical characteristics, typical habitat, social behaviors, and care of offspring; it concludes by offering the suggestions of scientists and conservationists for saving the species from extinction.

Because her students live in Wisconsin, far removed from tropical ocean waters, Ms. Dennison realizes that most of them have probably never seen manatees in the flesh. In an attempt to make the creatures more meaningful for them, she asks, "How big is a manatee compared to you?"

"It's bigger than us," Jon responds. "It's probably about the size of my mom or dad."

"It's about two of me," Marty says.

"No, I think it's more like three or four of us squashed together but a little taller," Keri suggests.

"Is a manatee like anything you've ever seen before, Keri?" Ms. Dennison asks.

"No...well, yeah...maybe," Keri replies. "It reminds me of a cow, only it lives in water. 'Cause it looks fat and is shaped like a cow's body, but it's just missing its legs."

"Excellent observation, Keri!" Ms. Dennison exclaims. "Did you know that manatees are sometimes called *water cows* or *seacows*? Adult manatees can grow to 12 or 13 feet in length and can weigh about 3,500 pounds. Unfortunately, because they usually live in such a polluted environment, most of them only grow to about ten feet in length and weigh about 1,000 pounds." Changing the subject, she continues. "The video told us that manatees come up to the water's surface to breathe air. But they don't have any legs, do they? So how do you think they move around in the water?"

"They use their flippers to swish themselves through the water," answers John.

"They use their tails to push themselves," adds Chase.

"When they're on the bottom, they use their flippers like legs," Keri suggests rather tentatively.

"Those are three very good hypotheses," Ms. Dennison observes. "Yesterday I went to the school library and borrowed a book about manatees. Chapter 3 tells us exactly how manatees move themselves around in the water. Who would like to read it aloud for us?"

After a lengthy discussion of manatees, Ms. Dennison says, "We need to have a system for keeping track of all the things we learn about each of the species we'll be studying." She draws her students' attention to a large matrix she has drawn on the chalkboard at the side of the room. The columns of the matrix are all labeled: *Species, Description, Habitat, Population Estimates, Feeding, Offspring, Social*

Behavior, and *Causes of Mortality*. She writes "manatees" in the *Species* column and then she and her students discuss what to write under each of the other headings.

Once the class has filled in the "manatees" row in the matrix, Ms. Dennison passes out black-and-white maps of the western hemisphere, depicting the borders of different countries as well as major rivers and mountain ranges. "We'll use these to indicate where each of our endangered species lives," she explains. "Take out your colored pencils, and use your blue pencil to color in the places where manatees live."

Two days later, Ms. Dennison introduces another endangered species—the loggerhead turtle. She shows a short videotape depicting the habitat and behaviors of loggerhead turtles and then says, "Let's fill in another row of our endangered species matrix." She writes "loggerhead turtles" in the *Species* column, then tapes a colorful picture of a loggerhead in the *Description* column.

"When we were studying manatees," Ms. Dennison says, "we learned a new vocabulary word that refers to where a species lives. Can anyone remember what that word was?"

"Habitat!" Sally shouts out.

Ms. Dennison nods her approval. "Yes, a species' *habitat* is the kind of environment in which members of the species typically live. For example, do they live on land or in water? Is the temperature warm or cold? If the species lives in water, is it fresh water or salt water? Is the habitat of loggerhead turtles the same as the habitat of manatees?"

"Loggerheads live where the manatees live, "responds Jon. "Around Florida, in the Caribbean Sea, and as far north as Canada."

"Hmmm...what do the rest of you think?" Ms. Dennison asks.

"They can't live near Canada," Jacinda responds. "'cause the water's too cold."

"I'm confused, Jacinda," Ms. Dennison says. "Who are *they*—the manatees or the turtles?"

"The manatees."

"Right! Manatees live only in warm water, but loggerhead turtles can live in either warm or cold water. And unlike manatees, who stay close to shore, sea turtles *migrate* to the open ocean, often traveling hundreds or even thousands of miles to a beach where they can lay their eggs. *Migrate* is a new vocabulary word. What do you suppose it means?"

"Move," answers Beth.

"Yes, *migrate* means to move from one place to another. A species often migrates with the seasons; for example, birds fly south in the fall and then fly back north again in the spring. It would be a good idea to write *migration* on your list of new vocabulary words for this week. Remember to write down a definition to help yourself remember what it means." She pauses to give the children time to write the new word in their notebooks.

"So loggerhead turtles *migrate*," Ms. Dennison continues. "Now pull out the maps of the western hemisphere that I gave you the other day. You've already colored your maps in blue for the manatees. Let's use the color red to mark where sea turtles live and migrate. Once we've found out where different endangered species live, we can start talking about how we might protect their environments so that they can grow and flourish."

NOTE: The following year, Ms. Dennison's class "adopted" a whale named Sophie, raising $5000 by selling T-shirts with Sophie's picture silk-screened on the front. A local television station televised their donation to the Wildlife Federation. The enterprise was so successful that adoptions of endangered species are now annual events at Ms. Dennison's school.

Possible question for "Endangered Species":

1.   *What strategies does Ms. Dennison use to promote her students' learning?*

CASE 41
The Research Paper

As Mr. Van Holten begins his fifth year teaching seventh-grade English, he reflects back on the worksheets and one-page compositions that he has assigned in previous years. He realizes that those assignments have had little relevance to the real-world tasks that his students will eventually face. He decides to assign a more meaningful, authentic task this year by asking his students to write ten-page research papers on topics of their choice, with the papers being due at the end of the school year.

Judging from past experience, Mr. Van Holten knows that some of his students will have limited writing skills, so he decides to ease his classes into the writing process with a series of short writing assignments. He begins fall semester by having his students write three sentences every day. He wants writing to be an enjoyable activity for his students, not an unpleasant one, so he refrains from giving them any feedback about spelling and grammar errors; instead, he simply puts checkmarks in his gradebook to indicate completed assignments.

After two weeks of daily sentence writing, Mr. Van Holten introduces a new task: During each class period, his students must write a short paragraph that has a topic sentence and at least three supporting sentences. Continuing to believe that negative feedback would dampen the students' motivation to write, he again provides no feedback about the quality of work that is produced.

Two weeks later, Mr. Van Holten changes the daily task once again. Each day, students must choose a specific topic and write three paragraphs about it. In addition, he now insists that everyone use correct spelling.

The following month, Mr. Van Holten asks his students to write a five-paragraph theme once a week. First drafts of these themes are due every Wednesday. On Thursday, the students exchange papers and check one another's work for mechanical errors. Final drafts are due at the beginning of class each Friday. Any spelling or grammatical errors on these final drafts lower a student's grade by 10%. Mr. Van Holten's students continue to write paragraph themes until the end of the semester.

On the first day of spring semester, Mr. Van Holten teaches his students how to use such references as encyclopedias, magazines, maps, CD-ROMs, and on-line resources. The following day, he describes the major assignment for the semester: a ten-page research paper that will be worth 75% of each student's final semester grade.

When many students express concern that they do not feel that they can produce such a long paper, Mr. Van Holten reassures them. "Of course you can do this assignment, folks. You spent all of last semester practicing the kind of writing that you will be doing. Besides, I'll give you lots of time during class to work on your papers, and you can go to the library whenever you need to."

Over the next few weeks, Mr. Van Holten notices that although some of his students are taking advantage of the allotted class time to work on their research papers, other students are wasting time socializing or completing homework for other classes. He decides to ignore the off-task behaviors, rationalizing that students must take responsibility for their own learning. If they don't finish their papers, then they will simply suffer the logical consequence—a failing grade.

On the day that the research papers are due, Mr. Van Holten receives an assortment of products from his students, including all of the following:

- Completed papers, either typed or handwritten, that meet the criteria he described at the beginning of the semester
- Uncompleted papers that are partially typed and partially handwritten
- Papers plagiarized from original sources
- Papers listing many unrelated facts written in the form of paragraphs
- Rambling compositions without any references
- Notes from the parents of several of the more "chatty" students explaining why the work is incomplete

Mr. Van Holten has no idea how he should grade his students' papers. Does he grade them solely on content? Should he also consider such factors as grammar and punctuation? Should he give the same credit for papers that are typed, handwritten, or a mixture of the two? He never explained that plagiarism was unacceptable, so should he penalize those students who have copied their papers word for word from library resources? He neglected to teach his classes how to use footnotes to reference the ideas of others, so should he deduct points when students didn't include references? Should he give the "chatty" students a few more days to complete their papers at home? Mr. Van Holten is at a complete loss as to what to do.

Possible questions for "The Research Paper":

1. *What mistakes does Mr. Van Holten make?*
2. *What strategies might Mr. Van Holten use to scaffold the difficult task that he has assigned?*
3. *What strategies might Mr. Van Holten use to keep students on task during the second semester?*
4. *In the early weeks of the school year, Mr. Van Holten gives his students no feedback about grammar and spelling. What are possible advantages and disadvantages of this no-feedback strategy?*
5. *How might students with special needs have performed on Mr. Van Holten's assignment?*
6. *How should Mr. Van Holten evaluate his students' papers?*
7. *Reliability is the extent to which a teacher assesses something consistently. How can Mr. Van Holten make sure that he reliably grades students' research papers?*

CASE 42
Under the Bleachers

Thad Buchanan, a senior at Monroe High School, has just learned that the local Kiwanis Club has awarded him a large scholarship to attend college next year, provided that he maintains the 3.0 average he currently has and earns at least a C in all of his classes. Thad knows that he will be the first member of his family to attend college. His parents are very proud of him, and he certainly doesn't want to let them down. But the new scholarship has him worried; he's been struggling in Ms. Ihlenfeldt's calculus class, and he's afraid that he's going to finish the year with a D.

Ms. Ihlenfeldt knows that the scholarship is very important to Thad because his parents can't possibly afford to send him to college, so she has gladly been giving him extra help after school every day. She's also been assigning extra problems for him to do on the weekends so that he can gain additional practice with concepts and procedures that seem to give him particular difficulty. Thad is grateful for Ms. Ihlenfeldt's assistance, and he works hard to make the most of both the tutoring and the homework assignments that she gives him.

The day of his first calculus test, Thad thinks he is prepared but doesn't want to take any chances. He writes all the formulas he thinks he will need on a small note card and then hides the card up his sleeve. As he begins the test, he realizes that he can remember the formulas on his own. But when he finishes, he slips out the note card just to double-check his work.

"Thad, what are you *doing*??!!" Ms. Ihlenfeldt is standing over him, and all of his classmates are looking in his direction.

"I...umm...I was just checking my answers. I swear I didn't use this during the test, Ms. Ihlenfeldt!"

"Yeah, right!" whispers Jill, who is sitting behind him.

"You're busted, man," Tyrone mutters. "You've been caught red-handed. You might as well admit it."

As Ms. Ihlenfeldt takes the note card from Thad's hand, he pleads, "I wasn't cheating! I swear it!"

"Hey, come on, Thad!" Quinton exclaims. "If you had a cheat sheet anywhere *near* the test, then you were cheating. Ms. Ihlenfeldt grades her tests on a curve. It's not fair for the rest of us to get bad grades just because you cheated."

"Yeah, Thad, what were you going to do—change your *wrong* answers?" Jason taunts.

"No, no! It wasn't like that. I was just checking my work!" Obviously very upset, Thad runs out of the room.

"Okay, everyone," Ms. Ihlenfeldt tells the class, "please get back to work and finish your tests. I'll deal with Thad after class."

"What's to deal with?" Stewart asks. "Everyone knows the school policy. Students who are caught cheating automatically flunk and have to take the course over. I know, 'cause it happened to me."

During her planning period the following hour, Ms. Ihlenfeldt goes in search of Thad. She knows him well enough to guess that he's gone out by the football field behind the school building. Sure enough, that is where she finds him, sitting alone under the bleachers with his head in his hands. Quietly, she sits down next to him.

"What happened, Thad?"

"I've blown it, haven't I?"

"I don't know yet. I know you were *ready* for the test. Why did you think you had to cheat?"

"Last night I panicked. I felt all this pressure. I just didn't want to let anyone down. So I brought a crutch. And now it's ruined me."

"*Who* didn't you want to let down?"

"You, my parents, my brothers and sisters, my Uncle Jake—everyone. All they keep saying is, 'Look at Thad. Isn't he great? The first Buchanan to go to college.' Why do I have to be the *first*?"

"Thad, I think that the person you let down the most is yourself. You're the one you've really hurt here."

"No, that's not true. I've let you down after all the time and help you've given me. I've let my family down after they've been so proud of me. Most of all, I've proven that I'm not good enough to go to college."

"Thad, you have proven to me time after time that you understand calculus very well. There was no doubt in my mind today that you would do well on the test. I wonder if maybe you actually set yourself up to fail here."

"What?"

"I wonder if maybe you were afraid of doing well—if maybe you thought that Buchanans don't belong in college."

"Yeah, I guess it's *true*. I mean, what makes me so special? I thought my education would be a slap in my dad's face...as if I'm better than he is somehow."

"You've had more educational opportunities than your parents had when they were your age, but that doesn't mean that you're better than they are. What it really means is that you've been more *fortunate*."

"Oh.... I guess I never thought of it that way."

"Why did you bring the note card, Thad?"

"I was afraid of letting everyone down."

"Any other reason?"

"I...I was afraid I'd pass. If I passed, then I'd be better than my family...my parents. I didn't want to insult them...you know, their lack of education and all."

Ms. Ihlenfeldt is astounded by Thad's ability to reflect on his own behavior. She probes him further. "Do you really think your parents would feel insulted if you were to get a college degree?"

"Yeah...well, no. I guess it sounds kinda stupid, doesn't it?"

"Thad, come back to my classroom after school. I'll let you take the test again, but without your note card this time."

"Is it really fair to the rest of the class? The school says I have to flunk."

"Thad, do you want to go to college?"

"Yes, more than anything."

"Why, Thad? *Why* do you want to go to college?"

"Because I want to prove to myself that I can do it...that I'm smart enough to get a college degree."

"Thad, the school policy is designed to teach students a lesson—that cheating is not in your own best interest over the long run. I think you've already learned that lesson."

"Thanks, Ms. Ihlenfeldt...for everything," Thad tells his teacher as he turns in his completed test. Once he's left the room, Ms. Ihlenfeldt grades his work. She's delighted to discover that he's earned an almost perfect score—96% correct.

NOTE: Four and a half years later, Thad graduated from M.I.T. with a degree in engineering. He now works for a computer firm in New England. He often writes to Ms. Ihlenfeldt to let her know how he is doing.

Possible questions for "Under the Bleachers":

1. *If you were Thad's teacher, would you allow him to retake the test? Why or why not?*

2. *Is it appropriate for schools to punish cheating in the way that Monroe High School does (i.e., by awarding an automatic F to all offenders)? Why or why not?*

3. *In general, what are the advantages and disadvantages of allowing students to retake an exam?*

4. *Criterion-referenced grades are based upon the student's mastery of a specific topic. In contrast, norm-referenced grades are based upon how well the student does as compared to the rest of the students in the class. Of the two, which of these ways does Ms. Ihlenfeldt grade her students?*

CASE 43
The Pearl

Mr. Hartman's eleventh-grade English class is reviewing for a test on the novel it's been reading the past two weeks, John Steinbeck's *The Pearl*. To help focus the review session, Mr. Hartman has written the following four terms on the board: "setting," "theme," "conflict," and "symbolism." Most of his students have their notebooks open in front of them, ready to take notes to which they can refer when they study this evening.

"We've talked about *setting* before, haven't we?" says Mr. Hartman. "It's when and where a story takes place. What's the setting for *The Pearl*?"

Trin Lee raises her hand. "It starts out in a small village, then ends up in the mountains. Because it's a parable, time doesn't exist. It takes place sometime in the past, but we don't know exactly when."

"Great answer, Trin Lee!" Mr. Hartman writes "village and mountains; time is in the past" to the right of "setting" on the board. He waits until his students have had time to copy what he's written into their notebooks, then asks, "Can anyone add anything to the setting?" When no one responds to his question, he says, "Okay, then let's discuss the theme of the story. Who can tell me what a *theme* is?"

"It's the main idea of the story—the underlying message," Rusty replies. "There's a 'C' word you used to describe it yesterday—'coots' or 'croots' or something like that."

"I think the term I used yesterday was *crux*," Mr. Hartman says as he writes the word on the board. *Crux* is another way of saying 'main idea.' So what is The *Pearl's* theme?"

"It's man's inhumanity to man," Loraine volunteers. "The pearl buyers are part of a conspiracy to cheat the divers out of their money. The doctor and the priest take advantage of the poor people."

"But there's more to it than that," Jean-Luc points out. "Steinbeck was talking about why materialism is so bad. I think he was warning us that we only hurt ourselves when we get greedy."

"You're on the right track, Jean-Luc," Mr. Hartman says. "Tell us a little bit more about what you mean."

"Well, Kino's search for wealth destroyed his happiness. He ruined his simple, happy life because of his greed."

"So in this novel we have two themes, peoples' inhumanity toward one other and the corruptive influence of materialism." Mr. Hartman writes both phrases on the board next to "theme," then continues. "Who can tell us about the *conflict* of the story?"

"I can," offers Meg. "The conflict is whether to trust your own judgment or go see what an expert thinks. For example, when the scorpion stung the baby, the parents knew what to do and they did it—they sucked the poison out of the baby's wound. Yet they weren't sure they did the right thing, so they went to the doctor afterwards to get his advice."

"So the conflict is 'trusting oneself versus trusting an expert'," Mr. Hartman says aloud as he writes the phrase on the board. "Finally, what are some of the *symbols* in the story?"

"Steinbeck use dark and light imagery," Daniel replies. "Light is symbolized as good, and darkness is symbolized as evil."

"True," says Mr. Hartman, "but what about the title of the book? What do you think the pearl is a symbol of?"

"It represents Kino's hopes and dreams," Rob replies. "He thinks that finding a pearl is the only way he can change his life. It's sorta like winning the lottery for us."

"Nice analogy, Rob," responds Mr. Hartman. "Do you think the pearl might also be a symbol of something else?"

"It's evil for Juan and Juana Tomas," Leigh suggests. "'Cause if Juan hadn't found the pearl, they'd probably still be happy."

"Good answer, Leigh!" Mr. Hartman replies as he writes "good and evil, hopes and dreams" on the board next to "symbolism." "It looks to me as if you people are ready for tomorrow's test. Any questions?" The students shake their heads and close their notebooks as the final bell rings.

The following day, Mr. Hartman waits for his students to clear their desks of everything but their pencils, then he hands out the test. "You have 35 minutes to take the test. There are ten matching items where you match people in the book with their personality traits. Then there are ten true-false items regarding things that did or did not happen in the story. After that, there are 20 multiple choice items related to specific details in the plot and ten more related to new vocabulary words."

A few minutes later, Loraine gets up and approaches Mr. Hartman's desk.

"Mr. Hartman, I don't understand this question," she whispers. She points to the following item on the second page:

When Kino looks at the pearl for the last time, he thinks it is:
>   a.   evil
>   b.   wonderful
>   c.   a dream
>   d.   a keepsake

"I have it in my notes that he sees the pearl both as evil and as a dream," Loraine continues. "So which letter should I circle?"

"I can't tell you that," Mr. Hartman says. "Just choose the best one."

"But they're *both* true!" she responds.

"You're wasting too much time on one question, Loraine. You only have ten minutes to finish the test. Why don't you leave this question for now and come back to it later if you have time?"

Obviously frustrated, Linda leaves her teacher's desk. Meanwhile, Elena walks to the front of the room. "Mr. Hartman," she says, "we never talked about this stuff." She points to an item at the bottom of the second page:

A real pearl is created by:

    a.   chemical transformation
    b.   a grain of sand
    c.   a grain of salt
    d.   a protective secretion

"It was in the novel, Elena," Mr. Hartman replies. "You'll have to figure it out by yourself." Elena shakes her head in disgust as she returns to her seat.

"Man, this is stupid!" Nellie whispers to Booker, who is sitting across the aisle beside her. "We never even discussed vocabulary words."

"I can't remember some of these characters," Booker whispers back. "They weren't important for the story, so we never talked about them in class."

"Hey, shut up, you guys!" Alex complains.

"Enough talking," Mr. Hartman admonishes the class. "Audrey, try to keep your eyes on your own paper. People, you're making this test harder than it needs to be. I'm not going to tell you any of the answers. I want you to stay in your seats and just try your best. You only have five more minutes to finish up, then we need to begin our discussion of *To Kill a Mockingbird*."

The following day, Mr. Hartman gives his students their graded test papers. "I'm not at all pleased with your test performance," he complains. "None of you did very well on the new vocabulary words that appeared in the novel."

"But we never expected anything about vocabulary on the test," Booker complains. "Like, who would know what *escarpment* means?"

"Well, now you know that you need to study new vocabulary words the next time we have a test," Mr. Hartman replies. "Many of you confused the pearl buyer and the doctor in the matching section—the doctor was the "selfish man" and the pearl buyer was the "shrewd appraiser," not the other way around. And all of you missed items 7 and 9 on the true-false. Fortunately, most of you did fine on the multiple choice questions."

"Since we all missed some of the same questions, are you going to throw them out?" asks Tobey.

"No, I want to base the test scores on 100 points," Mr. Hartman replies. "I can't do that if we throw out some of the questions."

"Mr. Hartman, I'm confused," Trin Lee says. "Why did we go over themes, symbolism, and stuff like that if the test was over picky details?"

"Well, it's a good idea to know that stuff. The test I gave you yesterday was specially designed by experts who had analyzed *The Pearl*. I knew it would be a better test than I could ever make up."

"So you didn't write the test yourself?" Trin Lee asks, seeking clarification.

"That's correct. I will be using tests written by the same experts for the other novels we read this semester. So if you didn't do as well as you'd like on this first test, at least you know what to expect on the next one."

Possible questions for "The Pearl":

1.   What effective instructional strategies does Mr. Hartman use during his lesson?
2.   Why does Rusty have trouble remembering the word crux?
3.   In what way does Rob contribute to the class's understanding of The Pearl?
4.   Validity is the extent to which an assessment tool actually assesses what it is intended to assess. Is Mr. Hartman's test a valid one? Why or why not?
5.   Reliability is the extent to which an assessment tool obtains the same result consistently. Is Mr. Hartman's test a reliable one? Why or why not?
6.   What other problems do you see in how Mr. Hartman administers the test?
7.   If you were Mr. Hartman, what other strategies might you use to have students demonstrate their understanding of The Pearl?

DATE DUE

SEP 0 4 1999			
FE 2 4 04			
GAYLORD			PRINTED IN U.S.A